COINS
OF THE
LAND OF ISRAEL

COLLECTION OF THE BANK OF ISRAEL
A CATALOGUE

ARIE KINDLER

Director, Kadman Numismatic Museum, Tel Aviv

Translated from the Hebrew by R. Grafman
Translation edited by Gabriel Sivan

KETER PUBLISHING HOUSE JERUSALEM LTD.

CONTENTS

CJ217
.B21
1974
GETS

FOREWORD

Like other central banks, the Bank of Israel decided in its early years to form a collection of coins, in this instance coins of Eretz Israel, namely, Jewish and related coins from ancient times. This decision stemmed mainly from Government policy regarding the modern coinage of the State of Israel from its very inception. For Israel's modern coins are a direct continuation of the ancient ones and their designs give new, maximal expression to the ancient designs. The coins issued today by the Bank of Israel display both this continuity and a freshness of spirit characteristic of our times, every effort being made to ensure an artistic and aesthetic design.

The Bank of Israel collection was begun with the purchase from the Bezalel National Museum of a series of Jewish coins, together with some local city coins of Eretz Israel. An additional purchase was made in 1963, comprising part of a Jewish coin collection that was offered for sale by Bank Leu & Co. and A. Hess of Lucerne, Switzerland. Apart from these two basic acquisitions —coins of the Jewish War against Rome, the War of Bar Kokhba, and the "Judaea Capta" series—the Bank of Israel has purchased individual coins so as to bridge gaps in various series. The collection has thus been built up within a relatively short space of time and we have been able to achieve a measure of completeness as far as these Jewish coins are concerned. In fact, this is now a fairly representative collection of Eretz Israel's ancient coinage.

Furthermore, the Bank of Israel has purchased most of the shekels and half-shekels discovered in the course of Prof. Yigael Yadin's excavations at Masada in 1963–65. These will appear first in Prof. Yadin's publications and are therefore not included in the present catalogue, but coins of the same type figure in the Bank's collection, as presented here.

With the issue of this catalogue, we feel bound to express our indebtedness to those who assisted in building up the Bank of Israel's coin collection: the late Mordechai Narkiss, a former director of the Bezalel National Museum, who laid the foundations of the present collection; the late Leo Kadman, former President of the Israel Numismatic Society, who served on the collection's Purchasing Committee; and the two other members of the Committee, Dr. Y. Meshorer and Mr. A. Kindler.

This catalogue was prepared at our request by Mr. Arie Kindler, Director of the Kadman Numismatic Museum (at the Museum Haaretz, Tel Aviv), and to him we express our appreciation. We must also thank all those who cooperated in this project: Dr. Ya'akov Meshorer, for preparing the coins; Mrs. Daliah Amotz, for the photographs; Mr. D. Genachovsky, for editing the catalogue; Mrs. Rachel Shapira-Kleiman and Mrs. Ramah Zuta, for preparing the material for press; and Mr. Y. M. Brin, who is in charge of the collection at the Bank of Israel as Director of the Currency Supply Unit.

We hope that this catalogue will serve as a valued reference work for numismatists, and as a handbook and source of inspiration for the general reader.

David Horowitz
Governor of the Bank of Israel
1971

AUTHOR'S PREFACE

This catalogue of the Coin Collection of the Bank of Israel was prepared at the request of the Bank Management. The pride of the Collection is the group of coins from the two Jewish Revolts against the Romans. Especially notable among the individual items are the "Yehud" coin, the tetradrachm of the first year of the Bar Kokhba Revolt, and the gold *Judaea Capta* issue. Besides the Jewish coins, the Collection includes a series of coins of the Roman procurators who ruled in Judea, and a series of *Judaea Capta* coins commemorating the Roman victory over the Jews—both of which occupy an important place in the numismatic documentation of the history of the Jewish people in its Land. The Collection also contains a group of coins minted at various periods by various cities in Eretz Israel. The catalogue opens with an electrum coin from the very dawn of minting in the ancient world, which originated in Asia Minor.

To facilitate use of the catalogue for the non-specialist, and to make it a book suitable for anyone interested in the history of the Jewish people, the actual numismatic sections and the numismatic terminology have been kept to a minimum, and are presented largely within the bibliography accompanying the description of each coin. This bibliography is based mainly upon four standard books, all of which are vital for the study of ancient Jewish coins: the works of G. F. Hill, M. Narkiss, A. Reifenberg, and Y. Meshorer (see the Bibliography on page 4).

This catalogue offers an innovation in the arrangement of ancient Jewish coins, presenting them, as they are displayed in the Bank of Israel Collection, in chronological order. The major problem in such a chronological arrangement concerns the Bar Kokhba coins, and we have devoted a special section to this matter, advising the reader of the various factors involved and of the solutions, which are based on the results of the most recent studies by specialists in this field.

The obverse ("head") of the coin has generally been fixed as that side which mentions the issuing authority, such as the high priest, king, emperor, prince (*nasi*, in the case of Bar Kokhba), or city (such as Jerusalem). For the bilingual coins, the obverse has been fixed as that side which bears the Hebrew legend.

I must thank the Bank of Israel and its Governor, who facilitated my work in preparing this catalogue by appreciating its value for historical and numismatic research; and the staff of the Bank of Israel who assisted me in the writing and editing, and in bringing the catalogue to press. I am also most grateful to the publishers and their staff for the pleasing design.

A. Kindler

BIBLIOGRAPHY

Bibliographical Abbreviations of Major Works

Narkiss—M. Narkiss, *The Coins of Palestine* I, *Jewish Coins,* Jerusalem, 1936 (Hebrew).

Narkiss II—M. Narkiss, *The Coins of Palestine* II, *The Coinage of the Gentiles,* Jerusalem, 1938 (Hebrew).

Reifenberg—A. Reifenberg, *Ancient Jewish Coins,* Jerusalem, 1940.

Meshorer—Y. Meshorer, *Jewish Coins of the Second Temple Period,* Tel Aviv, 1967.

Hill—G. F. Hill, *A Catalogue of the Greek Coins in the British Museum, Palestine,* London, 1914.

Kadman, *Jewish War*—L. Kadman, *The Coins of the Jewish War of 66–73 C.E. (Corpus Nummorum Palaestinensium,* III*)*, Jerusalem, 1960.

Symbols

N = Gold
R = Silver
E = Bronze

Note

For the convenience of the reader, legends in ancient Hebrew script are accompanied by their equivalent in modern ("square") Hebrew.

INTRODUCTION

Mediterranean civilization was relatively late in making use of coinage. Most scholars believe that, in the second half of the seventh century B.C.E., Lydian merchants first began stamping their marks on small ingots of standard weight and of a metal called electrum—a natural alloy of gold and silver found in the river Pactolus. These coins were intended to facilitate trade, since until then metal used as a means of payment had to be weighed out at each transaction. The trade-marks of these merchants—various animals, such as lions, bulls, rams, etc., or their heads—were often accompanied by the merchants' names, and served to guarantee the quality and weight of the metal. One such ingot-coin is in the Bank of Israel Collection (No. 1).

Coinage first reached Eretz Israel at a slightly later period; the earliest coins found in this country are Greek, dating from the second half of the sixth century B.C.E. The archaeological evidence indicates that, at least until the end of the period of the First Temple (586 B.C.E.), metal as a means of payment was weighed out with each transaction, and that the units of weight were the *shekel, neṣef, pym,* and *beka*ʿ; silver ingots in these weights have been found in the excavations at En-Gedi near the Dead Sea.

In the Persian Empire, too, coins were not in general use, though imperial coins were struck for the western satrapies, mainly those parts of Asia Minor having Greek settlements, where coinage had been in use for some time.

From the end of the fifth century B.C.E. until the era of Alexander the Great, the cities and kings of Phoenicia that were vassals of the Persian "King of Kings" issued silver coins in several denominations, the most famous of which was the double-shekel of Sidon. These coins, mainly from Sidon and Tyre, entered commercial use in Eretz Israel and became the principal means of payment in the northern districts and along the coast south to Joppa, in those regions granted to the king of Sidon by the Persian monarch.

At this same period local minting began, mainly in two regions, Judea and the Gaza district. These silver coins are quite rare, but the variety of types is indicative of the freedom granted to the imaginative and artistic talent of local die-cutters. In their designs and denominations such local issues were influenced by Greek and Eastern coins brought here by Phoenicians, mainly from Asia Minor. Since historical sources on this country for the century preceding the advent of Alexander the Great are very scanty, there is no way of knowing for certain to whom the issues should be ascribed, and the entire group of pre-Alexandrine silver coins is thus usually defined as "Greco-Phoenician."

A new era began with Alexander's conquest of Eretz Israel—the Hellenistic period. Under his successors, Eretz Israel was seized by the Ptolemaic rulers of Egypt in the third century B.C.E., and then by the Seleucid rulers of Syria in the second century B.C.E. Whether the régime was Egyptian or Syrian, the conqueror's coins became current in Eretz Israel and were often even struck here.

Only after the rise of an independent state under the Hasmoneans was an autonomous Jewish coinage struck in Eretz Israel. The first Jewish ruler to issue coins was John Hyrcanus I (135–104 B.C.E.), and autonomous Jewish coinage here came to an end with the suppression of the Bar Kokhba Revolt in 135 C.E. It is this period of 270 years of autonomous Jewish coinage that is best represented in the Collection of the Bank of Israel.

I. LYDIA

1. Electrum (natural alloy of gold and silver). 1/3 stater.
Seventh century B.C.E. 4.70 gr. 10/13 mm.

Obverse:

Lion's head to right, with mane and open mouth; on head, small intaglio markings in various forms, ancient assaying marks.

Reverse:

Two incuse rectangles containing unidentifiable forms.

This is one of the earliest coins minted.

Bibliography: B. V. Head, *Catalogue of the Greek Coins of Lydia in the British Museum,* London, 1901, Nos. 2–3.

II. JUDEA UNDER PERSIAN RULE

Although the land of Judea formed part of the Persian Empire during the sixth to fourth centuries B.C.E., it also came under the influence of Greek culture. Greek merchants reached the country at this time and even settled in coastal cities, such as Acre and Gaza, where their coins were regularly used. The most important of these coins, the Athenian tetradrachm, became the standard currency in the Eastern Mediterranean. On the obverse is the head of Pallas Athene, while the reverse bears an owl, the goddess' holy bird, and the legend: AΘE, an abbreviation of "Athens." The figure of the owl became widely familiar and local Oriental rulers, seeking to endow their coinage with a value comparable to that of Athens, continued to imitate the motif long after it had passed out of use in Athens itself. Among those who copied this design were the local authorities in Judea. The *Yehud* (Aramaic, "Judea") coins are on a far lower artistic level than those of Athens, and are distinguished by their script, for the letters Ɣ ℥ יהד (*Yehud*) appear in place of the Greek legend.

The *Yehud* coins are extremely rare, since their diminutive size often resulted in their loss. Today, several varieties of these coins have been classified; the type in the Bank of Israel Collection is unique, as it is the sole example bearing the head of Pallas Athene on the obverse. This is one of the earliest coins to be minted in Judea, although we do not know whether it was issued by the Persian authorities or by an autonomous or semi-autonomous authority there.

YEHUD

2. Æ obol. Fourth century B.C.E. (prior to Alexander the Great). 0.45 gr. 7/7.5 mm.

Obverse:
Head of Pallas Athene to right, wearing helmet.

Reverse:
Owl standing to right, with head facing front. Behind, at upper left, olive sprig. Legend, at upper right reading outward: Ɣ ℥ יהד (*Yehud*).

III. COINS OF THE HASMONEANS

The period of the Hasmoneans extended over some 130 years, from the Maccabean revolt in 167 B.C.E. until the murder of the last of the dynasty, Mattathias Antigonus, in 37 B.C.E. After the death of Antiochus IV Epiphanes in 163 B.C.E., the Seleucid dynasty of Syria began to decline, giving encouragement to the Hasmoneans in their ambition to renew the political independence of the Jewish people following the military successes of Judah Maccabee. It was Antiochus VII Sidetes who, according to 1 Maccabees 15:2–9, sent an epistle to Simeon, last of the Maccabee brothers and the first to achieve actual rule (142–135 B.C.E.), in which he specifically stated: ". . . I give thee leave also to coin money for thy country with thine own stamp. . . ."

Many scholars have tried to link the contents of this letter with various Jewish coins such as those bearing the name *Shim'on*, and especially those anonymous issues bearing the legend "Year four of the Redemption of Zion." However, it is clear today that none of these were minted by him. For while Antiochus VII did grant Simeon certain political privileges, in order to secure his assistance against Tryphon, the moment that Antiochus gained victory he hastened to withdraw those privileges before Simeon could issue coins of his own. The Hasmonean coins were therefore first issued only under Simeon's son, John Hyrcanus I (135–104 B.C.E.).

Most coins are dated according to the year of the issuing ruler's reign, the year of the Seleucid era, or the era of a particular city or of a particular war (as in the case of the two Jewish revolts); but with only one exception, the Hasmonean coins are all undated. This has led to difficulties in dating them and afixing their chronological order. An additional difficulty in this respect arises from the fact that different Hasmonean rulers went by the same name: thus, we find two named John Hyrcanus, and two named Judah Aristobulus.

The controversy over the ascription of these coins has not yet been resolved, and we cannot delve here into their detailed chronology. In the present catalogue we have used a chronological order based largely on paleographical considerations, according to which most of the coins bearing the name *Yehohanan* were minted by John Hyrcanus II. We may note that B. Kanael has concluded that the earliest Hasmonean coins were minted in 111/110 B.C.E., whereas Y. Meshorer regards Alexander Jannaeus as the first to issue coins.

The values of the Hasmonean coins are mostly small, i.e., perutah and half-perutah—corresponding to the Seleucid lepton and dilepton. The Hasmoneans struck no silver coinage, limiting their issues to bronze, and it seems likely that Seleucid silver coins and Tyrian Shekels and half Shekels were used in Eretz Israel for the higher values.

The legends on these coins are either monolingual or bilingual. The former are in Hebrew, using the early Hebrew script (like all other ancient Jewish coins); the bilingual coins have one side in Hebrew and the other in Greek, apparently to facilitate their use by both the Jewish and the non-Jewish populations of the country.

Strict adherence to the Second Commandment precluded the use of a ruler's portrait on Hasmonean coins, but motifs and emblems such as wreaths, stars, anchors, flowers (roses or lilies?), palm branches, helmets, cornucopiae and double cornucopia, and even ritual appurtenances from the Temple (the Table of Shewbread and the seven-branched *Menorah*), do appear. Some of the designs on these coins imitate those on Seleucid bronze coins dating from the latter half of the second century B.C.E.

no.11

JOHN HYRCANUS I (135–104 B.E.C.)

After the murder of Simeon, and the accession to the throne of his son, John Hyrcanus I, the latter's independence was at first rather limited. Antiochus VII revoked the political privileges extended to Simeon, invaded Judea, and besieged Jerusalem. He agreed to raise the siege in return for a payment of 500 talents and an undertaking to pay tribute for the cities held by John Hyrcanus I outside Judea, as well as for the surrender of hostages. For his part, John renewed old ties with the Senate of Rome in order to ensure his autonomous rule through Roman political pressure on Antiochus. It is assumed that the coin issued in 132–130 B.C.E. (No. 3) was intended by Antiochus for those areas held by John Hyrcanus I.

Only after the death of Antiochus VII was John Hyrcanus I freed from Seleucid overlordship. The Seleucid heir, Demetrius II, was forced to fight for his throne, and John took advantage of this opportunity to make conquests in Transjordan, Samaria, and Idumea. As Seleucid rule grew weaker, John's independence became more pronounced.

It is difficult to ascertain exactly when John Hyrcanus I began minting coins, but their issue was undoubtedly connected with the general political situation in the Middle East. Like the cities of Tyre (which began minting coins in 126/125 B.C.E.) and Ashkelon (which followed suit in 104/103 B.C.E.), it seems probable that John issued his first coinage between 126 and 104 B.C.E., since he was subject to the same Seleucid pressures and influences as those cities.

ANTIOCHUS VII SIDETES (138–129 B.C.E.)

3. Æ. 132–130 B.C.E. 2.60 gr. 14/15 mm.

Obverse:

Anchor, upside down.

Legend opposite, reading downward in three lines: [ΒΑΣΙΛΕΩΣ] ANTIOX[OY] EYEPΓETO[Y] (Of King Antiochus, Benefactor); at upper end of anchor, facing outward (worn on our example): AΠP (181 of the Seleucid era = 132/131 B.C.E.); BΠP (182 of the Seleucid era = 131/130 B.C.E.).

Reverse:

Pomegranate blossom (or lily?). Border of dots.

Coins of this type are found mainly in Judea, hence the assumption that they were minted for this region.

Bibliography: *Narkiss* II, No. 164; Danish National Museum, *Sylloge Nummorum Graecorum* (The Royal Collection of Coins and Medals), 35, *Syria, Seleucid Kings*, Copenhagen, 1959, No. 340.

JOHN HYRCANUS I

4. Æ. 1.65 gr. 13/16 mm.

Obverse:

Wreath tied at bottom, with leaves in groups of three.

Legend within, in four lines (fourth line off flan in our example):

יהוח
בן הכה(ן)
(הגד)ול וח(בר)
(היהודים)

(Yehoḥanan the High Priest and the *Ḥever* of the Jews).

Reverse:

Double cornucopia with pendant ribbons; within, pomegranate. Border of dots.

Bibliography: *Narkiss*, No. 6; *Reifenberg*, No. 10; *Meshorer*, No. 26; *Hill*, p. 194, No. 40.

JUDAH ARISTOBULUS I (104–103 B.C.E.)

Upon the death of John Hyrcanus I, Judah Aristobulus I succeeded to the throne. Against his father's express wishes that he be given only the position of High Priest (political control remaining with his mother), Aristobulus also seized the reins of government and according to Josephus, in order to secure his throne, he imprisoned his mother and brothers. He was the first Hasmonean to style himself "king" (though only for internal purposes; on his coins, he merely retained the title of high priest). During his short reign, Judah Aristobulus concentrated his political activities on the settlement of Jews in Galilee and the conquest of part of the land of Yattir.

5. Æ. 1.90 gr. 13/14 mm.

Obverse:
Wreath tied at bottom, with leaves in groups of three.
Legend within, in five lines:

	יהוד
	ה כהן גד
	ול וחבר
	היהוד
	ים

(Judah the High Priest and the *Ḥever* of the Jews).

Reverse:
Double cornucopia, with pendant ribbons; within, pomegranate. Border of dots.

Bibliography: *Narkiss*, No. 9; *Reifenberg*, No. 13; *Meshorer*, No. 28; *Hill*, p. 197, Nos. 1–3.

13

ALEXANDER JANNAEUS (103–76 B.C.E.)

When Judah Aristobulus I died, his widow Salome Alexandra (Shlomzion) freed her brothers-in-law from prison and married one of them—Alexander Jannaeus. Like his predecessors, Jannaeus initially styled himself "high priest" on his coinage, but later he did not hesitate to glorify himself with the title of king.

During his reign the traditional, monotonous style of the Hasmonean coins was altered. The coins on which Alexander Jannaeus styled himself "high priest" were struck in the traditional form, i.e., with a wreath surrounding the legend and a double cornucopia on the reverse. But all the coins of the "Yehonathan the King" series bear, apart from the Hebrew, a Greek legend apparently intended to emphasize Jannaeus' importance among his non-Jewish subjects. It is with these coins of Alexander Jannaeus that we first encounter internal chronological problems. It is most probable that he at first continued to strike coins in the tradition of his predecessors, bearing the legend "Yehonathan the High Priest and the *Hever* of the Jews." The *Hever* may refer to the Sanhedrin, or to the Assembly of Elders of the People, or to some other elected body not mentioned in the ancient sources.

Alexander Jannaeus later instituted the "Yehonathan the King" series, first of the type depicting a star in a circle and an anchor, later also with a star and an anchor in a circle (in perutah and half-perutah values, some bearing dates), and finally of the type with a flower and an anchor in a circle, the half-perutah coin bearing a palm branch and a flower.

With the last of his coins, Jannaeus returned to the traditional type: the legend within a wreath and a double cornucopia. Since this latter type is often struck over the flower/anchor in a circle, the type with a flower/anchor in a circle must be the latest of the "Yehonathan the King" series.

These later coins of the "High Priest" series, struck over coins of the "Yehonathan the King" series and others of the same type, are paleographically of a different sort and reduced the usual form of the name "Yehonathan" to "Yonathan"; this may have been an attempt by Jannaeus to come to terms with his Pharisee rivals toward the end of his life, whereby he not only relinquished his royal title but also avoided the formula of the Tetragram at the beginning of his name (*Yeho-*).

There are also lead coins of Alexander Jannaeus, with one face always quite clear, resembling the anchor in a circle (of the flower/anchor in a circle type), while the other face is generally blank (or obliterated). Recently, the Aramaic legend on these coins was deciphered, reading: "King Alexander." These coins are also of the "Yehonathan the King" series, and are quite rare; they seem to have been issued for only a short period during some temporary economic crisis.

FIRST "HIGH PRIEST" SERIES

6. Æ. 1.80 gr. 14 mm.

Obverse:

Wreath tied at bottom, with leaves in groups of three.
Legend within, in five lines:

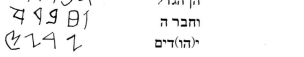

(י)הו

נתן הכ(ה)

ן הגדל

וחבר ה

יה(וד)י(ם)

(Yehonathan the High Priest and the *Ḥever* of the Jews).

Reverse:

Double cornucopia, with pendant ribbons; within, pomegranate.
Border of dots. Struck off-center.

Bibliography: *Narkiss*, No. 10; *Reifenberg*, No. 20; *Meshorer*, No. 12; *Hill*, pp. 204–207, Nos. 39–60.

7. Æ. 2.20 gr. 14/15 mm.

Obverse:

Wreath tied at bottom, with leaves in groups of three.
Legend within, in five lines:

יהו

(נ)תן הכ

הן הגדל

וחבר ה

י(הו)דים

(Yehonathan the High Priest and the *Ḥever* of the Jews).

Reverse:

Double cornucopia, with pendant ribbons; within, pomegranate.
Border of dots. Struck off-center.

Bibliography: *Narkiss*, No. 10; *Reifenberg*, No. 20; *Meshorer*, No. 12; *Hill*, pp. 204–207, Nos. 39–60.

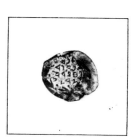

15

"YEHONATHAN THE KING" SERIES

8. Æ. 3.00 gr. 15/16 mm.

Obverse:
Eight-rayed Star surrounded by knotted fillet.
Legend, between rays: בֿ‎ ﬠ‎ + ﬠ‎ TH‎ ל (מל/כ)/ה/נ/ת/ן/הו/י
(Yehonathan the King).
Struck off-center.

Reverse:
Anchor. Border of dots.
Legend, around from lower left: ΒΑΣΙΛΕΩΣ ΑΛΕΞΑΝΔΡΟΥ
(Of King Alexander).

Bibliography: *Narkiss*, No. 11; *Reifenberg*, No. 14; *Meshorer*, No. 8; *Hill*, p. 207, No. 61.

9. Æ. perutah. 1.95 gr. 14 mm.

Obverse:
Eight-rayed Star. Border of dots.
Legend, outside border in Aramaic script, part of: מלכא אלכסנדרוס שנת כ"ה
(King Alexander, Year 25). = ca. 78 B.C.E.
Struck off-center.

Reverse:
Anchor upside down within circle; dots at points of anchor.
Legend, around circle: ΒΑΣΙΛ[ΕΩΣ ΑΛΕΞΑΝΔ]ΡΟΥ
(Of King Alexander). Almost entirely worn on this specimen.

Bibliography: *Narkiss*, No. 12; *Reifenberg*, No. 15; *Meshorer*, No. 9; *Hill*, pp. 210–211, Nos. 1–18.

10. Æ. 1.30 gr. 13/15 mm.

Obverse:

Eight-rayed Star. Border of dots.

Legend, around border in Aramaic script: סולכא מלכא

מלכא אלכסנדרו[ס שנת כ"ה (King Alexander, Year 25).   =   ca. 78   B.C.E.

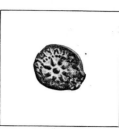

Reverse:

Anchor upside down within circle; dots at points of anchor.

Legend, around circle: ΒΑΣ[ΙΛΕΩΣ ΑΛΕΞ]ΑΝΔ (Of King Alexander).

Bibliography: *Narkiss*, No. 12; *Reifenberg*, No. 15; *Meshorer*, No. 9; *Hill*, pp. 210–211, Nos. 1–18.

11. Æ. 1.40 gr. 13 mm.

Obverse:

Lily flower. Border of dots.

Legend, around from left below: יהונתן המלך

(Yehonathan the King).

Reverse:

Anchor upside down within circle.

Legend, around circle from lower left:

ΒΑΣΙΛΕΩΣ ΑΛΕΞ[ΑΝΔΡΟΥ] (Of King Alexander).

Bibliography: *Narkiss*, No. 13; *Reifenberg*, No. 16; *Meshorer*, No. 5; *Hill*, p. 198, Nos. 1–8.

12. Æ perutah. 2.40 gr. 15 mm. Struck over flower/anchor type.

Obverse:
Wreath tied at bottom, with leaves in groups of three.
Legend, within, in five lines:

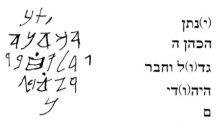

(י)נתן
הכהן ה
גד(ו)ל וחבר
היה(ו)די
ם

(Yehonathan the High Priest and the *Ḥever* of the Jews).
Traces of previous striking: Greek letters (around anchor and circle).

Reverse:
Double cornucopia, with pendant ribbons; within, pomegranate. Border of dots.
Clear traces of previous striking: lily flower, border of dots.
Legend: יהונתן ה(מלך) (Yehonathan the King).

Bibliography: *Narkiss*, No. 14; *Reifenberg*, No. 18; *Meshorer*, No. 17; *Hill*, pp. 199–202, Nos. 11–29.

13. Æ perutah. 3.30 gr. 15/17 mm. Struck over flower/anchor type.

Obverse:
Wreath tied at bottom, with leaves in groups of three.
Legend within, in unknown number of lines: ינתן הכהן הגדל וחבר היהודים
(Yehonathan the High Priest and the *Ḥever* of the Jews).
Traces of previous striking: Greek letters and circle around anchor:
ΝΔΡΟΥ ΒΑΣ.

Reverse:
Double cornucopia, with pendant ribbons; within, pomegranate. Border of dots.
Traces of previous striking: flower.

Bibliography: *Narkiss*, No. 14; *Reifenberg*, No. 18; *Meshorer*, No. 17; *Hill*, pp. 199–202, Nos. 11–29.

14. Æ perutah. 2.40 gr. 14/16 mm.

Obverse:

Wreath tied at bottom, with leaves in groups of two.
Legend within, in five lines:

ⵣⴹ⳧ⴳ	יהונ
ⵝⴷⵌⵅ	תן הכהן
ⵐ⳧⳽ⴷⵍ	הגדל וח
ⵥⴶⵍ⳦	בר הי(הודי)
ⵍ	ם

(Yehonathan the High Priest and the *Ḥever* of the Jews).
Rather crude execution.

Reverse:

Double cornucopia, with pendant ribbons; within, pomegranate. Border of dots. Struck off-center.

Bibliography: *Meshorer*, No. 16.

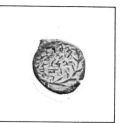

15. Æ perutah. 1.70 gr. 13/14 mm.

Obverse:

Wreath tied at bottom, with leaves in groups of three.
Legend within, in four lines, in imitation script:

ⵍ ⵗ ⴷ/ⵜⵊ
ⵔ ⴹ ⵝⵏⵔⵜⵜ
ⵝⵌⵉⵌⵊ ⵉ ⴷⵜ
ⵊⵗⵚ ⵗ

Reverse:

Double cornucopia, with pendant ribbons; within, pomegranate. Border of dots.

Bibliography: *Meshorer*, No. 16.

JOHN HYRCANUS II (67, 63–40 B.C.E.)

Upon the death of Alexander Jannaeus, Salome herself took over the reins of government, while the office of high priest was given to her son, John Hyrcanus II. Under Salome, power was actually in the hands of the Pharisees. It is not known whether coins were issued by this queen, but one view holds that the coins bearing a large Greek alpha above the name of Yehoḥanan the High Priest were struck in conjunction with his mother, the queen, whose Greek name was Alexandra.

When Salome died, her sons, John Hyrcanus the High Priest and Aristobulus II, quarreled. It can be assumed that the Hebrew name of this Aristobulus was Judah, like that of his uncle Judah Aristobulus I. The civil war continued for four years until the Roman Consul Pompey intervened in 63 B.C.E., marking the first Roman penetration into Judea. Pompey conquered Jerusalem and even dared to enter the holy of holies in the Temple. He himself left intact the privileges of John Hyrcanus II as High Priest. Shortly after, however, Gabinius, the Roman consul of Syria, did interfere in the State affairs of the Hasmonean Kingdom, whose decline had already begun. Gabinius removed many Hellenistic cities from "the yoke of Jewish rule" and, in the northern part of the country, he founded the Decapolitan league. He also left his mark on the internal organization of the Hasmonean state, dividing it into five *Sanhedriyot* (districts). At this period, Antipater the Idumean— father of Herod the Great—served as an adviser to John Hyrcanus II.

Two Roman Republican denarii bear witness to this stormy period. When Marcus Scaurus, one of Pompey's generals, interfered in the Hasmonean internecine struggle, he forced the retreat of the Nabatean king Aretas III, who had been supporting Hyrcanus. In commemoration of this event, he struck a coin in 58 B.C.E. depicting the vanquished king kneeling before a camel and waving a palm branch in token of his desire for peace. A coin of similar description, bearing the legend: BACCHIVS IVDAEVS, was issued by the Aedile Aulus Plautius in 54 B.C.E. It can be assumed that this legend (BACCHIVS IVDAEVS) refers to the Dionysius mentioned by Josephus as being the ruler of Tripoli at this period. If so, this coin indicates that Dionysius was a Jew. Narkiss has conjectured that the coin is an indication of the unsuccessful insurrections of Aristobulus and his son Alexander, which occurred in the same year. When the civil war ended in Rome, Julius Caesar restored some of his former privileges to John Hyrcanus II, and even appointed him "Ethnarch."

Paleographic research, together with other data, has helped to ascertain that a large number of the coins bearing the name "Yehoḥanan" were indeed issued by John Hyrcanus II. The patterns on most of his coins are in the tradition of his predecessors. He also minted half-perutahs and even a larger coin, apparently in the value of one and a half perutahs (trilepton). On some of his coins, he is referred to as "Head of the *Ḥever* of the Jews," and it is assumed that these coins were issued by him after he had received the title of ethnarch. A few of his coins bear such monograms as A or AΠ on their reverse.

JOHN HYRCANUS II

JOINT ISSUE WITH SALOME ALEXANDRA(?)

16. Æ perutah. 1.75 gr. 13/14 mm.

Obverse:
Wreath tied at bottom, with leaves in groups of three.
Legend within, in five lines:

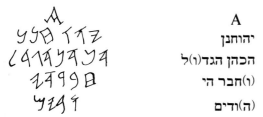

	A
	יהוחנן
	הכהן הגד(ו)ל
	(ו)חבר הי
	(ה)ודים

(A[lexandra?] Yehoḥanan the High Priest and the *Ḥever* of the Jews).

Reverse:
Double cornucopia, with pendant ribbons; within, pomegranate.
Border of dots.

Bibliography: *Narkiss*, No. 5; *Reifenberg*, No. 8; *Meshorer*, No. 19; *Hill*, pp. 188–190, Nos. 2–14.

no. 17

ISSUE OF THE AEDILE AULUS PLAUTIUS

17. Æ denarius. Ca. 54 B.C.E. 3.90 gr. 18 mm.

Obverse:
Head of goddess Cybele to right, wearing turreted crown and earring, hair partly knotted and partly falling on neck. Border of dots.
Legend, from upper right: A. PLAVTIVS; from upper left, reading outward: AED. CVR. S.C. Assayer's mark: incuse S.

Reverse:
Bearded figure in robes kneeling beside camel, raising hand with palm branch as token of peace. Border of dots.
Legend, below: [B]ACCHIVS; on right, reading outward: IVDAEVS.

Bibliography: M. Narkiss, in *Tarbiz* 11/2, pp. 220–223 (Hebrew); E. Sydenham, *The Coinage of the Roman Republic*, London, 1952, No. 932; A. Kindler, "Two Republican Denarii illustrating contemporary events," in *Seaby's Coin and Medal Bulletin*, Feb. 1951, pp. 53–55.

18. Æ perutah. 2.20 gr. 14 mm.

Obverse:

Wreath tied at bottom, with leaves in groups of three.
Legend within, in four lines:

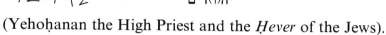

יהוחנן
הכהן הגד(ו)
ל וחבר ה
יה(ו)דים

(Yehoḥanan the High Priest and the *Ḥever* of the Jews).

Reverse:

Double cornucopia, with pendant ribbons; within, pomegranate. Border of dots. Struck off-center.

Bibliography: *Narkiss,* No. 6; *Reifenberg,* No. 9; *Meshorer,* No. 18; *Hill,* pp. 190–194, Nos. 15–44.

19. Æ perutah. 2.10 gr. 14 mm.

Obverse:

Wreath tied at bottom, with leaves in groups of three.
Legend within, in five lines:

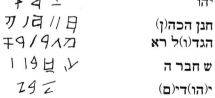
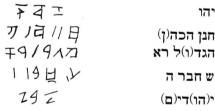

יהו
חנן הכה(ן)
הגד(ו)ל רא
ש חבר ה
י(הו)די(ם)

(Yehoḥanan the High Priest, Head of the *Ḥever* of the Jews).

Reverse:

Double cornucopia, with pendant ribbons; within, pomegranate. Border of dots. Struck off-center.

Bibliography: *Narkiss,* No. 7; *Reifenberg,* No. 11; *Meshorer,* No. 22.

20. Æ half-perutah. 1.15 gr. 10/11 mm.

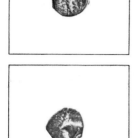

Obverse:
Upright palm branch.
Legend, parallel to and flanking branch, from top to bottom.
On left inward in two lines:

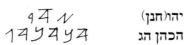
יהו(חנן)
הכהן הג

On right outward in two lines:

ד(ו)ל החבר
היה(ו)ד(י)ם

(Yehoḥanan the High Priest and the *Ḥever* of the Jews).

Reverse:
Lily flower. Border of dots.

Bibliography: *Narkiss*, No. 8; *Reifenberg*, No. 12; *Meshorer*, No. 21; *Hill*, pp. 195–196, Nos. 48–56.

no. 16

MATTATHIAS ANTIGONUS (40–37 B.C.E.)

Mattathias Antigonus, the last of the Hasmoneans, was a unique personality. In the wake of the Hasmonean civil war, he had been taken to Rome, but escaped in 55 B.C.E. and returned to the Land of Israel. Here he was caught and again sent back by Gabinius, the Roman governor of Syria. In Rome, he was freed and came a second time to this country. All the while, John Hyrcanus II was ruling as high priest with Antipater as his adviser; the latter purposely undermined Hyrcanus' rule with the aim of replacing him on the throne of Judea with his own son, Herod. In 42 B.C.E., Mattathias attempted a coup d'état with the aid of his brother-in-law, Ptolemy Mennaeus, but was defeated by Herod. His second attempt, with the help of the Parthians in 40 B.C.E., was successful. Mattathias held sway in Judea but was involved in constant warfare with Herod until 37 B.C.E. Mattathias lacked the strength, however, to withstand his rival, since Herod had already obtained the support of Rome in 40 B.C.E., when he was formally installed on the throne of Judea. Mattathias' execution in Antioch in 37 B.C.E. put an end to the Hasmonean dynasty.

Mattathias Antigonus' struggle finds expression in his coins, as he was the only one of his dynasty to make serious changes in the Hasmonean coin types. Not only did he issue large values, he also struck coins with purely Jewish symbols, such as the Table of Shewbread and the *Menorah* (seven-branched candlestick). Furthermore, his coins help to unravel the mystery surrounding his Hebrew name, as the ancient sources mention only his Greek name, Antigonus. Most of his coins bear bilingual legends; the difference between them and those of Alexander Jannaeus, however, lies in the fact that the latter styled himself "king" in both Hebrew and Greek, whereas Mattathias Antigonus only called himself "king" in Greek, using the title "High Priest" in Hebrew.

21. Æ "large bronze" (di-chalcous). 14.80 gr. 24 mm.

Obverse:
Double cornucopia. Border of dots.
Legend, around from lower left, and within cornucopia:

מתתיה כהן גדל חבר (ה)י(הו)ד(ים) ⌐ꓓ𐤗𐤗 Ꝑ 𐤀 ⅄𐤄𐤁𐤂𐤋 𐤀𐤃 𐤁𐤂𐤋𐤔𐤓

(Mattathias the High Priest and the *Ḥever* of the Jews).

Reverse:
Wreath tied at bottom, with leaves in groups of two. The ends of the ribbon stand up within the wreath.
Legend, around from lower right, reading outward:
ΒΑΣΙΛΕΩΣ ΑΝΤΙΓΟΝΟΥ (Of King Antigonus).

Bibliography: *Narkiss*, No. 17; *Reifenberg*, No. 21; *Meshorer*, No. 30; *Hill*, pp. 212–215, Nos. 2–21.

22. Æ "half" (chalcous). 7.50 gr. 18 mm.

Obverse:

Cornucopia, with pendant ribbon on right and bunch of grapes hanging on left. Border of dots.

Legend, around from lower left: ꓒꓥꓩ ꓷꓕꓥꓩꓘꓬ ꓫꓷꓫꓫꓬ (מתתיה כו(ה)ן (ג)דל חבר ה(יהודים) (Mattathias the High Priest and the *Ḥever* of the Jews).

Reverse:

Wreath tied at left, with leaves in groups of three. Border of dots.

Legend within, in three lines: BACIΛ/EOCAN/TIΓO (Of King Antigonus).

Bibliography: *Narkiss*, No. 18; *Reifenberg*, No. 22; *Meshorer*, No. 31; *Hill*, pp. 216–217, Nos. 35–55.

23. Æ perutah. 1.50 gr. 14 mm.

Obverse:

Wreath, with leaves in groups of three. Border of dots.

Legend within, in two lines from left to right (retrograde!) מתתיה (Mattathias).

Reverse:

Double cornucopia, with ribbons; within, ear of barley. Border of dots.

Bibliography: *Narkiss*, No. 19; *Reifenberg*, No. 25; *Meshorer*, No. 33; *Hill*, p. 219, Nos. 57–59.

24. Æ perutah. 1.30 gr. 14/15 mm.

Obverse:

Table of Shewbread (non-perspective view). Border of dots.

Legend, around from lower left reading outward, around border: (מתת)יה כוהן ג(דול) (Mattathias the High Priest).

Reverse:

Menorah on flat base.

Legend, around from lower right reading outward: [ΒΑΣΙΛΕ]ΩΣ ΑΝ[Γ.] (Of King Antigonus).

Bibliography: *Narkiss*, No. 20; *Reifenberg*, Nos. 23–24; *Meshorer*, No. 36; *Hill*, p. 219, No. 56.

IV. COINS OF THE HERODIAN DYNASTY

The Herodian dynasty ruled over the various parts of Eretz Israel for a period of 137 years (37 B.C.E. until about 100 C.E.). The founder of the dynasty was Antipater, adviser to John Hyrcanus II; its first actual ruler, however, was Herod ("the Great"). Herod's extensive kingdom was divided between his three sons after his death. His grandson, Agrippa I, succeeded for a time in restoring some of the splendor of the kingdom, reuniting many of his grandfather's territories. The last ruler of the dynasty, Agrippa II, ruled over lands distant from Jerusalem, in the northern part of the country.

The Herodian coins display a gradual retreat from Jewish tradition. Herod himself no longer used Hebrew legends on his coins, retaining only the Greek; however, with a few exceptions, designs that would not offend Jewish religious feelings were employed.

Herod's son, Philip, went a stage further, striking coins bearing not only the portrait of the Roman emperor, but also his own portrait and a depiction of the temple of Augustus at Paneas, although he refrained from showing the deity within, as was commonly done on coins. Agrippa I proceeded to mint coins with his own portrait, as did his brother and nephew, the rulers of Chalcis in the Lebanon, and his son, Agrippa II, early in his reign. The greatest divergence from Jewish tradition is found in the coins of Agrippa II, which systematically portray the Flavian emperors, with goddesses such as Tyche and Nike on the reverse. Nor did he hesitate to issue coins of the "Judaea Capta" form.

This dynasty, too, issued only bronze coinage, but its coins were suited to the local economic situation; in form and value they resembled the other bronze coins current at this period.

HEROD THE GREAT (37–4 B.C.E.)

Herod was handed his kingdom in Judea by a decree of the Roman Senate, with the approval of Octavian (Augustus), in 40 B.C.E. At that time, Mattathias Antigonus was in control of the country, and Herod found himself obliged to wrest the land from this last ruler of the Hasmonean dynasty; he succeeded in doing so with Roman assistance in 37 B.C.E. In order to enhance his status within the accepted Jewish royal family, Herod married Mariamne, the granddaughter of John Hyrcanus II, in that same year. A wily politician, Herod always knew which way the wind was blowing and which power to turn to for aid; he thus became a close friend of Augustus, the Roman emperor. An ambitious king, Herod ruled over many territories and his building activities throughout his kingdom and beyond have become famous: He built Sebaste (Samaria) and founded Caesarea in honor of Augustus, also erecting theaters and temples here and there. His crowning achievement in this direction, however, was the rebuilding of the Temple in Jerusalem, the splendor of which is still reflected in the mighty stones of the Western and Southern Walls of the Temple Mount. These numerous activities did not, however, endear him to the people, for his reign was marred by many acts of cruelty, which did not spare even his own family: his wife, two of his sons, and many others were murdered by him. His friendly relations with the Roman emperor strengthened Roman influence in Eretz Israel, and the results are obvious from the first century C.E. down to the Arab conquest in the seventh century.

The coins of Herod bear no symbols offensive to Jewish religious feelings, except possibly for the eagle (see No. 38), with which he adorned the Temple façade. Several of the motifs appearing on his coins, such as the cornucopia and the anchor, were adopted from Hasmonean coins, and thus were acceptable to the Jews *a priori*. The legends were henceforth entirely in Greek, describing Herod as "king." Many of the patterns have reference to the sea (galley, aphlaston, and anchor); to war (helmet and shield); and to cult (tripod and thymiaterion, or incense burner, both probably deriving from the Temple).

In the coinage of Herod there are again chronological problems. Only one series, artistically the finest, is dated – to the third year of his reign; this is generally considered to be 37 B.C.E., the year in which he finally succeeded in taking control of the country (if one dates his reign from 40 B.C.E., the year in which the Roman Senate handed him the throne). The remainder of his coins are undated and there is no way of unravelling their chronological order.

25. Æ chalcous. 37 B.C.E. 6.10 gr. 22/23 mm.

Obverse:

Tripod on base, with bowl (ritual furnishing in the Temple?). Border of dots.
Legend, around from upper right: ΒΑΣΙΛΕΩΣ ΗΡΩΔΟΥ (Of King Herod);
in field on left: LΓ (3rd year of Herod's reign, 37 B.C.E.); in field on right,
indecipherable ligature: ℞.

Reverse:

Thymiaterion (a type of incense burner) surmounted by a star flanked by
palm branches (ritual object from Temple?). Border of dots.

Bibliography: *Narkiss,* No. 26; *Reifenberg,* No. 26; *Meshorer,* No. 37; *Hill,* pp. 220–221,
Nos. 1–10.

26. Æ hemi-chalcous. 37 B.C.E. 5.10 gr. 19/20 mm.

Obverse:

Crested helmet with cheek-pieces. Border of dots.
Legend, around from the upper right: ΒΑΣΙΛΕΩΣ ΗΡΩΔΟΥ (Of King
Herod); in field to left LΓ (3rd year of Herod's reign, 37 B.C.E.); in field to
right, indecipherable ligature: ℞.

Reverse:

Circular shield. Border of dots.

Bibliography: *Narkiss,* No. 27; *Reifenberg,* No. 27; *Meshorer,* No. 38; *Hill,* p. 224, Nos. 11–13.

27. Æ trilepton. 37 B.C.E. 3.00 gr. 16/18 mm.

Obverse:

Winged caduceus, symbolic of Hermes and of trade, wealth, and prosperity.
Border of dots.
Legend, around from upper right: ΒΑΣΙΛΕΩΣ ΗΡΩΔΟΥ (Of King Herod);
in field to left: LΓ (3rd year [of Herod's reign, 37 B.C.E.]); in field to right,
indecipherable ligature: ℞.

Reverse:

Pomegranate on branch with several leaves. Border of dots.

Bibliography: *Narkiss,* No. 28; *Reifenberg,* No. 28; *Meshorer,* No. 39; *Hill,* pp. 221–222,
Nos. 14–17.

28. Æ perutah. ?7 B.C.E. 2.70 gr. 14/15 mm.

Obverse:

Aphlaston (bow ornament of galley in shape of bird's wing). Border of dots.
Legend, around from upper left: ΒΑΣΙΛΕΩΣ ΗΡΩ[ΔΟΥ] (Of King Herod);
in field to left: LΓ (3rd year [of Herod's reign, 37 B.C.E.]); in field to right,
indecipherable ligature: ₽.

Reverse:

Upright palm branch between two leaves (?). Border of dots.

Bibliography: *Narkiss*, No. 29; *Reifenberg*, No. 29; *Meshorer*, No. 40; *Hill*, p. 222, Nos. 18–19.

29. Æ trilepton. 37 B.C.E. 17/18 mm.

Obverse:

Winged caduceus, symbolic of Hermes and of trade, wealth, and prosperity.
Border of dots.
Legend, around from upper right: [ΒΑ]ΣΙΛΕΩΣ ΗΡΩΔ[ΟΥ] (Of King Herod).
Without date of issue and ligature.

Reverse:

Pomegranate on stem with several leaves. Border of dots.
This example bears no date or ligature on the obverse, as is found on Nos.
25–28.

30. Æ perutah. 37 B.C.E. 2.50 gr. 15/17 mm.

Obverse:

Aphlaston (bow ornament of galley in shape of bird's wing). Border of dots.
Legend, around from upper right: ΒΑΣΙΛΕΩΣ ΗΡΩΔΟΥ (Of King Herod).

Reverse:

Upright palm branch between two leaves (?). Border of dots.
This example bears no date or ligature on the obverse, as is found on Nos.
25–28.

31. Æ trilepton. 3.20 gr. 19 mm.

Obverse:

Cross within fillet. Border of dots.

Legend, around from upper right: B[ΑΣΙΛΕΩΣ] ΗΡΩΔΟΥ (Of King Herod).

Reverse:

Tripod with curved legs and bowl, flanked by upright palm branches. Border of dots.

Bibliography: *Narkiss*, No. 25; *Reifenberg*, No. 30; *Meshorer*, No. 41; *Hill*, pp. 222–224, Nos. 20–39.

32. Æ trilepton. 2.30 gr. 17 mm.

Obverse:

Cross within fillet. Border of dots.

Legend, around: ΒΑΣΙΛΕΩΣ ΗΡΩΔΟΥ (Of King Herod).

Reverse:

Tripod with legs bent to sharp angles and bowl, flanked by upright palm branches. Border of dots (ritual object from Temple?)

Bibliography: *Narkiss*, No. 25; *Reifenberg*, No. 30; *Meshorer*, No. 41; *Hill*, pp. 222–224, Nos. 20–39.

33. Æ perutah. 1.50 gr. 15/17 mm.

Obverse:

Fillet. Border of dots.

Legend, around from upper right (mostly missing): ΒΑΣΙΛΕΩΣ ΗΡΩΔΟΥ (Of King Herod).

Reverse:

Tripod with curved legs and bowl (ritual object from Temple?). Similar to No. 32. Border of dots.

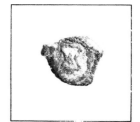

Bibliography: *Narkiss*, No. 25; *Reifenberg*, No. 32; *Meshorer*, No. 42; *Hill*, pp. 222–224, Nos. 20–39.

34. Æ half-perutah. 0.70 gr. 11/13 mm.

Obverse:
Tripod with curved legs (ritual object from Temple?). Border of dots.
Legend, around from upper right: [BACI]ΛCVC[HPΩΔHC] (Of King Herod).

Reverse:
Palm branch upright with large, spreading leaves. Border of dots.

Bibliography: *Meshorer,* No. 47.

35. Æ perutah. 1.50 gr. 13/15 mm.

Obverse:
Anchor. Border of dots.
Legend, around from upper right: BACI HPW (Of King Herod).

Reverse:
Double cornucopia, with pendant ribbons; within, caduceus. Border of dots.

Bibliography: *Narkiss,* No. 21; *Reifenberg,* No. 33; *Meshorer,* No. 53; *Hill,* pp. 224–226, Nos. 40–65.

36. Æ perutah. 0.90 gr. 12/15 mm.

Obverse:
Border of dots.
Legend, in three lines: [B]ACI
                      [ΛE]ΩCH
                      [PΩΔOY] (Of King Herod).

Reverse:
Anchor in circle; around, V-shaped ornaments.

Bibliography: *Narkiss,* No. 23; *Reifenberg,* No. 35 (different); *Meshorer,* No. 51; *Hill,* p. 226, Nos. 66–69.

37. Æ half-perutah. 0.80 gr. 12/13 mm.

Obverse:
Anchor.
Legend, around from upper left reading outward: UWH—scattered letters representing BACI HPW (Of King Herod).

Reverse:
Galley with aphlaston, oars, and ram. Border of dots.

Bibliography: *Narkiss*, No. 23; *Reifenberg*, No. 36; *Meshorer*, No. 55; *Hill*, p. 227, Nos. 75–77.

38. Æ half-perutah. 0.60 gr. 12/14 mm.

Obverse:
Cornucopia. Border of dots.
Legend, flanking from bottom to top: on left BACIΛ; on right HPWΔ (Of King Herod).

Reverse:
Eagle standing to right. Border of dots.

Bibliography: *Narkiss*, No. 24; *Reifenberg*, No. 34; *Meshorer*, No. 54; *Hill*, p. 227, Nos. 70–74.

39. Æ half-perutah. 0.60 gr. 11/12 mm.

Obverse:
Cornucopia. Border of dots.
Legend, flanking from bottom to top: on left: BACIΛ; on right: HPWΔ (Of King Herod).

Reverse:
Eagle standing to right. Border of dots.

Bibliography: *Narkiss*, No. 24; *Reifenberg*, No. 34; *Meshorer*, No. 54; *Hill*, p. 227, Nos. 70–74.

33

HEROD ARCHELAUS (4 B.C.E.–6 C.E.)

Following the death of Herod and the division of his kingdom, Archelaus received the major and most important share of territory, encompassing Samaria, Judea, and Idumea. He was also granted the title of ethnarch, earlier conferred on John Hyrcanus II by Julius Caesar. Archelaus ruled over an increasingly hostile population and, after ten years of his rule, a Jewish delegation went to Rome and complained to Augustus about Archelaus' oppressive regime. Augustus exploited the opportunity to make further inroads into Judea, banishing Archelaus and replacing him in 6 C.E. by a Roman procurator (Coponius); Archelaus' territories were annexed to Provincia Syria, with a special internal status.

Archelaus used his family name—Herod—on his coins, and it is only because of the associated title ("Ethnarch") that they can be identified as his rather than his father's. He also refrained from upsetting the Jews by avoiding emblems offensive to their religious feelings. Most of his motifs are subjects such as the galley, prow, and anchor; there are other patterns, however, such as the cornucopia, wreath, helmet, and the bunch of grapes (similar to the golden bunch present in the Temple in his father's day). Archelaus' coins are undated and their chronological order is therefore unknown; they are arranged here according to the motifs.

40. Æ perutah. 0.95 gr. 13/14 mm.

Obverse:

Anchor. Border of dots.

Legend, around from lower left (haphazard order): [HP]W Δ[OY] (Of Herod).

Reverse:

Double cornucopia, with pendant ribbons; within, caduceus. Border of dots. Legend, around from lower left (haphazard order): [EΘ]N[A]P[XOY] (Of the Ethnarch); the N is situated above the caduceus and between the cornucopiae.

Bibliography: *Narkiss*, No. 21, *Reifenberg*, No. 33A; *Meshorer*, No. 56; *Hill*, p. 226, Nos. 62–63.

41. Æ trilepton. 3.10 gr. 18/19 mm.

Obverse:

Double cornucopia jugate to left, with pendant ribbons; on left, hanging bunch of grapes. Border of dots.

Legend, around from upper right: HPWΔHC (Herod).

Reverse:

Galley to left, with high aphlaston, five oars, rudder, battering ram, and cabin on deck. Border of dots.

Legend, in field above in three lines (boustrophedon): EΘN/XPA/H (Ethnarch).

Bibliography: *Narkiss,* No. 36; *Reifenberg,* No. 53; *Meshorer,* No. 59A; *Hill,* p. 231, Nos. 1–6.

42. Æ perutah. 0.90 gr. 13 mm.

Obverse:

Double cornucopia jugate to right, with pendant ribbons; on right, hanging bunch of grapes. Border of dots.

Legend, around from upper right: HPWΔOY (Of Herod).

Reverse:

Galley to left, with high aphlaston, four oars, rudder, battering ram, and cabin on deck. Border of dots.

Legend, in field above in two lines: EΘN/A (Ethnarch).

Bibliography: *Narkiss,* No. 36; *Reifenberg,* No. 54; *Meshorer,* No. 60; *Hill,* p. 232, Nos. 7–9.

43. Æ perutah. 1.50 gr. 13/15 mm.

Obverse:

Prow with ram, to left. Border of dots.

Legend, around from bottom upward to right: HPW (retrograde) (Of Herod).

Reverse:

Wreath, with leaves in groups of two. Border of dots.

Legend within, in one line: EΘN (Ethnarch).

Bibliography: *Narkiss,* No. 38; *Reifenberg,* No. 56; *Meshorer,* No. 58; *Hill,* pp. 233–234, Nos. 27–37.

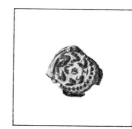

44. Æ perutah. 1.10 gr. 14/15 mm.

Obverse:
Anchor with especially long arms. Border of dots.
Legend, around from lower left (haphazard): HPW[Δ]OY (Of Herod).

Reverse:
Wreath tied at bottom, with leaves in groups of two; above, a kind of medallion closing the wreath.
Legend within, in two lines (boustrophedon): EΘ/AN (Ethnarch).

Bibliography: *Narkiss*, No. 39; *Reifenberg*, No. 57; *Meshorer*, No. 57; *Hill*, pp. 234–235, Nos. 38–43.

45. Æ perutah. 1.95 gr. 15/17 mm.

Obverse:
Vine branch with hanging bunch of grapes; small leaf at left. Border of dots.
Legend, in quarter circle from upper left to right: HPWΔOY (Of Herod).

Reverse:
Plumed helmet with cheek-pieces; below left, small caduceus. Border of dots.
Legend below, reading inward: [EΘ]NAPXOY (Of the Ethnarch).

Bibliography: *Narkiss*, No. 37; *Reifenberg*, No. 55; *Meshorer*, No. 61; *Hill*, pp. 232–233, Nos. 10–25.

no. 41

HEROD ANTIPAS (4 B.C.E.–39 C.E.)

After the division of Herod's kingdom, Antipas received Galilee together with Perea, a strip along the eastern bank of the River Jordan – a much smaller share than that received by his brother Archelaus. His portion, and that of Philip, were considered to encompass roughly one quarter of the total area of Herod's kingdom, and thus they were called "tetrarchies," and their rulers "tetrarchs." The two regions of Antipas' kingdom were not contingent, and he fixed his seat in Galilee, at first at Sepphoris and later (around 19/20 C.E.) at Tiberias, which he had founded.

Antipas was destined to play a role in the events of the New Testament and, where there is mention of "Herod," this almost invariably refers to him. It was he who executed John the Baptist, and it was to him that Pontius Pilate sent Jesus for interrogation.

After the death of the Emperor Tiberius, and with the accession of Caligula in 37 C.E., Antipas' wife Herodias urged him to request the Roman emperor to grant him the title of "king." The request did not meet with a favorable response. Agrippa I, the grandson of Herod and a boon companion of Caligula's son who lived for many years in Rome proper, was quick to press his own royal claims to Eretz Israel, and it is clear that he was secretly able to frustrate his uncle Antipas' ambitions, since his influence at the Roman court was decisive in the matter. Antipas was finally banished to Lugdunum (Lyons) in Gaul after various charges had made him appear as a traitor in the eyes of Rome.

Most of Antipas' coins are of a single type, bearing only floral patterns – a palm-tree, a palm branch, a bunch of grapes, or a wreath. Like his brother Archelaus, Antipas invoked his family name, "Herod," but the title of tetrarch accompanying it reveals the proper ascription of the coins. There are no chronological difficulties in regard to his coinage, for all of it is dated; the first coins bear the date of the 24th year of his reign (19/20 C.E.) and the last, his 43rd year (38/39 C.E.). Nor is there any doubt as to the place of minting, for all coins except those of his last year bear the city-name "Tiberias." The last issues, though, give the name and titles of Caligula – apparently instead of the imperial portrait which appears on the city-coins and on the issues of other vassal rulers.

46. Æ medium bronze. 29/30 C.E. 6.30 gr. 18 mm.

Obverse:
Upright palm branch. Border of dots.
Legend, around from lower left: ΗΡΩΔΟΥ ΤΕΤΡΑΡΧΟΥ (Of Herod the Tetrarch); in field flanking: LΛΓ (33rd year [of Antipas' reign, 29/30 C.E.]).

Reverse:
Wreath tied at bottom, with leaves in groups of two. Border of dots.
Legend within, in two lines: TIBE/
                          PIAC (Tiberias).

Bibliography: *Narkiss*, No. 32; *Reifenberg*, No. 45; *Meshorer*, No. 67A· *Hill*, p. 229, No. 1.

47. Æ large bronze. 38/39 C.E. 11.95 gr. 20/22 mm.

Obverse:
Palm-tree with seven branches and two bunches of dates. Border of dots.
Legend, in semi-circle downward from right to left:
[ΗΡΩ]ΔΗC ΤΕΤΡΑΡΧΗC (Herod the tetrarch); in field flanking: ΕΤΟ ΜΓ (43rd year [of Antipas' reign, 38/39 C.E.]).

Reverse:
Wreath tied at bottom, with leaves in groups of two. Border of dots.
Legend within, in four lines: ΓΑΙΩ
                        KAICAP
                        ΓΕΡΜΑ
                        NIKΩ (Caius Caesar Germanicus [Caligula]).

Bibliography: *Narkiss*, No. 35; *Reifenberg*, No. 50; *Meshorer*, No. 74.

48. Æ medium bronze. 38/39 C.E. 6.60 gr. 16/18 mm.

Obverse:
Upright palm branch. Border of dots.
Legend, around from lower left: [ΗΡ]ΩΔ[ΗC ΤΕΤΡΑΡΧΗC] (Herod the tetrarch); in field flanking: L ΜΓ (43rd year [of Antipas' reign, 38/39 C.E.]).

Reverse:
Wreath tied at bottom, with leaves in groups of two. Border of dots.
Legend within, in four lines: ΓΑΙΩ/KAICAP/ΓΕΡΜΑ/ΝΙ (Caius Caesar Germanicus [Caligula]).

Bibliography: *Narkiss*, No. 33; *Reifenberg*, No. 51; *Meshorer*, No. 73; *Hill*, p. 230, No. 10.

no. 50

HEROD PHILIP (4 B.C.E.–34 C.E.)

Philip was the third of Herod's sons to receive a portion of his kingdom – the regions of Trachonitis, Gaulanitis, and Batanea (Argob, Golan, and Bashan), that is, the north-eastern parts of the kingdom. Philip fixed his seat at Paneas (Banias), the city in which his father established a splendid temple in honor of Augustus Caesar. Philip developed the city and named it Caesarea, in honor of Augustus; in contradistinction to Caesarea Maritima, built by his father on the Mediterranean coast, this city was known as Caesarea Philippi.

A considerable proportion of the inhabitants of Philip's tetrarchy were non-Jews, and this may have led him to permit the minting of coins which differed in their design from those customarily struck by Jewish rulers until that time. Here we find not only the imperial portrait, but even a depiction of the Temple of Augustus at Paneas and also occasionally his own portrait. Like his brother Antipas, Philip styled himself "tetrarch," but he used his own name – Philippus – on the coins, rather than that of his family. On one coin he is described as the "founder" (KTIC[τη ς]), alluding to the refounding of Paneas as Caesarea Philippi. His coins, too, are dated throughout; the dates of his regnal years appear between the columns of the temple façade. Several of his coins bear round, incuse countermarks; some of these marks show a star, while others present ligatures that are difficult to interpret.

49. Æ medium bronze. 15/16 C.E. (?). 4.95 gr. 18/21 mm.

Obverse:

Head of Tiberius to right. Border of dots.
Legend, around from left below: [TI]BEP[IOC CEBACTOC KAICAP] (Tiberius Augustus Ceasar).
On neck, incuse countermark with ligature.

Reverse:

Tetrastyle temple façade with gable; dot in center of gable pointing to an ornament. Border of dots.
Legend, around from upper left reading outward: [ΦΙΛΙΠΠ]ΟΥ [ΤΕΤΡΑΡΧΟΥ] (Of Philip the Tetrarch); between columns: LI(?) (probably 19th year [of Philip's reign, 15/16 B.C.E.]). (Much of the depiction and legend on the reverse was destroyed during the punching of the countermark on the obverse.)

Bibliography: *Reifenberg*, No. 40 (?); *Meshorer*, No. 80A (?).

50. Æ medium bronze. 26/27 C.E. 6.80 gr. 18/19 mm.

Obverse:

Head of Tiberius to right, with olive sprig before him. Border of dots.
Legend, around from left below: TIBEPIOC CEBACTOC KAICAP (Tiberius Augustus Caesar).

Reverse:

Tetrastyle temple façade with gable; dot in center of gable pointing to an ornament. Border of dots.
Legend, around from right above reading outward: ΕΠΙ ΦΙΛΙΠΠΟΥ ΤΕΤΡΑΡΧΟΥ (Of Philip the Tetrarch); between columns: LΛ (30th year [of Philip's reign, 26/27 C.E.]).

Bibliography: *Narkiss*, No. 31A; *Reifenberg*, No. 41; *Meshorer*, No. 81A; *Hill*, p. 228, No. 3.

AGRIPPA I (37–44 C.E.)

As Herod's grandson, Agrippa I was educated at the imperial court in Rome. His friendship with Caligula and Claudius enabled him to secure the title of "king" and territories in Eretz Israel, which speedily expanded to the point where his kingdom almost matched that of his grandfather. Despite these ties with Rome, Agrippa's two attempts at a more independent policy were frustrated by Marsus, the Roman governor of Syria. The fortifying of Jerusalem with a stout wall was suspended by imperial command, and the summoning of a conference of vassal kings at Tiberias was dispersed by Marsus. Agrippa was particularly honored by his subjects because he was the grandson of Mariamne the Hasmonean and became religiously observant. He died suddenly at Caesarea in 44 C.E., at the age of 54.

Agrippa I struck two types of coin: The first (Nos. 51–53) was intended for Judea and bears a canopy and ears of barley; the other type was intended for those areas under his control where the majority of the population was non-Jewish, and these coins therefore display a more pagan character. The latter bear the portrait of Claudius, a temple, and a quadriga. Agrippa was the first of the Herodian kings who dared to strike his own portrait on his coins; on several he styles himself "King Agrippa the Great, Friend of Caesar." His coins are dated.

51. Æ perutah. 42/43 C.E. 2.40 gr. 18 mm.

Obverse:

Canopy on shaft. Border of dots.

Legend, around from upper right: [ΒΑCΙ]ΛΕWC ΑΓΡΙΠΑ (Of King Agrippa).

Reverse:

Three ears of barley stemming from between two leaves. Border of dots.

Legend, in field flanking: LS (6th year [of Agrippa's reign, 42/43 C.E.]).

Bibliography: *Narkiss*, No. 40; *Reifenberg*, No. 59; *Meshorer*, No. 88; *Hill*, pp. 236–237, Nos. 1–18.

52. Æ perutah. 42/43 C.E. 1.05 gr. 13 mm.

Obverse:

Canopy on shaft. Border of dots.

Legend, around from upper right: [ΒΑCΙΛΕWC ΑΓΡΙΠΑ] (Of King Agrippa).

Reverse:

Three ears of barley stemming from between two leaves. Border of dots.

Legend, in field flanking: [L]S (6th year [of Agrippa's reign, 42/43 C.E.]). Identical to No. 51, but much smaller than usual.

Bibliography: *Narkiss*, No. 40; *Reifenberg*, No. 59; *Meshorer*, No. 88; *Hill*, pp. 236–237, Nos. 1–18.

53. Æ perutah. 42/43 C.E. 0.85 gr. 13/14 mm.

Obverse:

Canopy on shaft. Border of dots.

Legend, around from upper right: [ΒΑCΙΛΕWC ΑΓΡΙΠΑ] (Of King Agrippa).

Reverse:

Three ears of barley stemming from between two leaves. Border of dots.

Legend, in field flanking: [LS] (6th year [of Agrippa's reign, 42/43 C.E.]). Identical to No. 51, but much smaller than usual.

Bibliography: *Narkiss*, No. 40; *Reifenberg*, No. 59; *Meshorer*, No. 88; *Hill*, pp. 236–237, Nos. 1–18.

54. Æ large bronze. 43/44 C.E. 16.20 gr. 25/26 mm.

Obverse:
Laureate head of Claudius to right. Border of dots.
Legend, around from upper right: TIBEPIOC [KAICAP] CEBACTOC
(Tiberius Caesar Augustus).

Reverse:
Façade of distyle temple with gable; within temple, four figures, two near
columns facing inward, upper half of third figure between them; fourth
figure below, nude, seated bent over. The right and middle figures wear
togas over their heads; the left figure wears a tunic. The outer figures hold
round objects (bowls or wreaths?); the upper middle figure holds a cylindrical
object (modius?).
Legend, around from upper right:
BAΣIΛEY[ΣMEΓAΣ] AΓPIΠΠAΣ ΦIΛO[KAIΣ]AP (The Great King
Agrippa, Friend of Caesar); within gable: LZ (7th year [of Agrippa's reign,
43/44 C.E.]). Double strike.

Bibliography: *Narkiss*, No. 48; *Reifenberg*, No. 60; *Meshorer*, No. 89A; *Hill*, p. 238, No. 23.

55. Æ medium bronze. 44 C.E. 6.70 gr. 18/19 mm.

Obverse:
Diademed head of Agrippa I to right. Border of dots.
Legend, around from lower left:
[BACIΛEYC MEΓAC AΓPIΠΠAC ΦIΛOKAICAP] (The Great King
Agrippa, Friend of Caesar).

Reverse:
Laureate Tyche standing to left, holding palm branch in left hand and rudder
in right hand. Border of dots.
Legend, around from upper right:
[KAICAP]IA H ΠPOC TΩ CEBACT[Ω ΛIMENI]   (Caesarea near the
port of Sebaste); in field to right: L[H] (8th year [of Agrippa's reign, 44 C.E.]).

Bibliography: *Narkiss*, No. 42; *Reifenberg*, No. 62; *Meshorer*, No. 92; *Hill*, p. 237, No. 20.

no. 57

AGRIPPA II (50–100 C.E.)

At the time of Agrippa I's death, his son Agrippa II was 17 years old. Various factors apart from the boy's age led the Roman authorities to withhold the succession from him, for toward the end of his reign Agrippa I had lost favor at the Roman court. Here was an opportunity to restore the former political status in Eretz Israel, and Roman procurators were once more despatched to the country. In 50 C.E., Agrippa II did manage to secure his throne, however, as King of Chalcis in the Lebanon. Three years later, he was granted the tetrarchy of his uncle, Philip, in place of Chalcis, as well as the eastern half of Galilee. He then fixed his seat at Caesarea Philippi, renaming it Neronias, after the emperor Nero.

The length of his reign enabled him to issue many different coin types. They display no Jewish affinities and, like his father, Agrippa II issued coins with his own portrait (No. 56). Most of them resemble the city-coins issued at the same period, generally bearing the portrait of the current emperor together with Tyche or Nike on the reverse. His coins also include types reminiscent of the local "Judaea Capta" series, indicative of his total dependence upon Rome. Most of his coins bear Greek legends, with a minority in Latin.

Although all of Agrippa II's coins are dated, serious chronological problems are involved; it is generally accepted that he denoted two different eras on them. The first was the era beginning in 56 C.E., and the second that beginning in 61 C.E.; the latter appears only in the small group of coins bearing Latin legends (Nos. 66–67).

UNDER NERO

56. Æ large bronze. 61 C.E. 11.30 gr. 23 mm.

Obverse:
Laureate head of Nero to right. Border of dots.
Legend, around from upper right: [NEPΩN KAICAP ΣEBAΣTOY] (Nero Caesar Augustus).

Reverse:
Circle within wreath tied at bottom, with leaves in groups of three. Border of dots.
Legend, within circle in five lines: ΕΠΙ
                                        ΒΑCΙΛΕ
                                        ΑΓΡΙΠΠ
                                        ΝΕΡΩ
                                        ΝΙΕ

(By King Agrippa, Nero). The last letter of the legend (E) indicates the date of issue (= 5th year [of Agrippa II's reign, 61 C.E.]).

Bibliography: *Narkiss*, No. 58; *Reifenberg*, No. 79; *Meshorer*, No. 95; *Hill*, p. 239, No. 1.

57. Æ small bronze. 66 C.E. 4.60 gr. 15/17 mm.

Obverse:
Bust of Agrippa II to left. Border of dots. Oval countermark behind neck, containing laureate head to left.
Legend, around from left below: [ΒΑΣΙΛΕΩΣ ΑΓΡΙ]ΠΠΟΥ (Of King Agrippa).

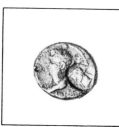

Reverse:
Anchor. Border of dots.
Legend, in field flanking: LI (10th year [of Agrippa II's reign, 66 C.E.]).

Bibliography: *Narkiss*, No. 52; *Reifenberg*, No. 75; *Meshorer*, No. 98.

UNDER VESPASIAN

58. Æ large bronze. 83 C.E. 18.60 gr. 27 mm.

Obverse:
Laureate head of Vespasian to right. Border of dots.
Legend, around from upper right:
ΑΥΤΟΚΡΑ[ΟΥΕCΠΑCΙ ΚΑΙCΑΡΙ] CΕΒΑCΤW
(Emperor Vespasian Caesar Augustus).

Reverse:
Tyche, goddess of fortune, standing to left, with calathos (?) on head, draped, holding cornucopia in left hand and ears of corn (?) in right hand. In field in upper left, a star.
Legend, in field flanking, in two lines: [E]ΤΟV ΚΖΒΑ/ΑΓΡΙ ΠΠΑ including date of issue (27th year [of the reign of] King Agrippa II [83 C.E.]).

Bibliography: *Narkiss*, No. 59; *Reifenberg*, No. 84; *Meshorer*, No. 106; *Hill*, p. 241, Nos. 13–14.

ISSUES WITH PORTRAIT OF TITUS

59. Æ medium bronze. 82 C.E. 9.80 gr. 25/27 mm.

Obverse:
Laureate head of Titus to right. Border of dots.
Legend, around from upper right: ΑΥΤΟΚΡ ΤΙΤΟC ΚΑΙCΑΡ CΕΒΑCΤΟC (Emperor Titus Caesar Augustus).

Reverse:
Nike, goddess of victory, striding to right, draped, holding wreath in raised right hand and palm branch in left hand, reaching to shoulder. Border of dots.
Legend, in field flanking in two lines: ΕΤΟ ΚϚ Β[Α]/ΑΓΡΙ ΠΠ[Α], including date of issue (26th year [of the reign of] King Agrippa II [82 C.E.]).

Bibliography: *Narkiss*, No. 61; *Reifenberg*, No. 91; *Meshorer*, No. 115; *Hill*, pp. 241–242, Nos. 19–24.

60. Æ medium bronze. 85 C.E. 12.50 gr. 23 mm.

Obverse:

Laureate head of Titus to right. Border of dots.

Legend, around from upper right: AYTOK[P TITOC KAI]CAP CEBAC
(Emperor Titus Caesar Augustus).

Reverse:

Nike striding to right, draped, holding wreath in raised right hand, and
palm branch reaching shoulder in left hand. Border of dots.

Legend, in field flanking in two lines: ETO KΘBA/AΓP[I] ΠΠA including
date of issue (29th year [of the reign of] King Agrippa II [85 C.E.]).

Bibliography: *Narkiss*, No. 61; *Reifenberg*, No. 93; *Meshorer*, No. 117; *Hill*, p. 242, Nos.
25–26.

ISSUE WITH PORTRAITS OF TITUS AND DOMITIAN

61. Æ large bronze. 22.12 gr. 29 mm.

Obverse:

Laureate heads of Titus and Domitian in confrontation.

Legend, around from lower left:

AVTOKP KAICAP TITOC K ΔO[METIANOC] (Emperor Caesar Titus
and Domitian).

Reverse:

The god Pan striding to left, holding pedum (shepherd's crook) on left
shoulder; tree-stump on left. Border of dots.

Legend, around from lower left: BACIΛEWC AΓPIΠΠ[AC] (Of King
Agrippa).

This coin is unique; the depiction of Pan here may indicate that it was minted
at Paneas.

Bibliography: *Meshorer*, No. 119; Monnaies et Médailles S.A., Basle, *Vente publique* 32
(20 octobre 1966), No. 211.

ISSUES WITH PORTRAIT OF DOMITIAN

62. Æ minor bronze. 81 C.E. 1.40 gr. 11/12 mm.

Obverse:

Laureate head of Domitian to right. Border of dots.

Legend, around from left below: [KAI ΔOMITI] (Caesar Domitian).

Reverse:

Cornucopia. Border of dots.

Legend, in field flanking in two lines: ET KE/BA AΓ including date of issue (25th year [of the reign of] King Agrippa II [81 C.E.]).

Bibliography: Stella Ben-Dor, in *BIES* 16 (1951), p. 60; A. Kindler, in *BIES* 18 (1953), p. 93 (both Hebrew); *Meshorer*, No. 131.

63. Æ small bronze. 82 C.E. 4.65 gr. 19/20 mm.

Obverse:

Laureate head of Domitian to right. Border of dots.

Legend, around from lower left: [K]AICAP ΔOMITIANOC (Caesar Domitian).

Reverse:

Nike, goddess of victory, standing to right, draped, with left foot on helmet, writing on shield resting upon left knee; star above, on right. Border of dots.

Legend, around from left below: ETO KS BA AΓPIΠΠA including date of issue (26th year [of the reign of] King Agrippa II [82 C.E.]).

Bibliography: *Narkiss*, No. 62; *Reifenberg*, No. 107; *Meshorer*, No. 134; *Hill*, pp. 244–245, Nos. 40–48.

64. Æ large bronze. 85 C.E. 14.00 gr. 25/27 mm.

Obverse:
Laureate head of Domitian to right. Border of dots.
Legend, around from lower left: [ΑΥΤΟΚΡ ΔΟΜ]ΚΑΙCΑΡ ΓΕΡΜΑΝΙΚ
(Emperor Domitian Caesar Germanicus).

Reverse:
Tyche, goddess of fortune, standing to left, with calathos (?) on head, draped, holding cornucopia in left hand and ears of corn (?) in right hand. Border of dots.
Legend, in field flanking in two lines: ΕΤΟΥ ΚΘ Β[Α]/[Α]ΓΡΙ ΠΠ[Α] including date of issue (29th year [of the reign of] King Agrippa II [85 C.E.]).

Bibliography: *Reifenberg*, No. 111; *Meshorer,* No. 138.

65. Æ large bronze. 86 C.E. 18.30 gr. 26/28 mm.

Obverse:
Laureate head of Domitian to right. Border of dots.
Legend, around from lower left:
[ΑΥΤΟΚΡΑ ΔΟΜΙΤΙΑΝΟC] ΚΑΙCΑΡ ΓΕΡ (Emperor Domitian Caesar Germanicus).

Reverse:
Tyche standing to left, with calathos (?) on head, draped, holding cornucopia in left hand and ears of corn (?) in right hand.
Legend, in field flanking in two lines: ΕΤΟΥ Λ ΒΑ/[Α]ΓΡΙ ΠΠΑ including date of issue (30th year [of the reign of] King Agrippa II [86 C.E.]).

Bibliography: *Meshorer*, No. 144; *Bulletin of the Israel Numismatic Society* 1 (Jan. 1967), No. 3, p. 58 (Hebrew).

ISSUES WITH PORTRAIT OF DOMITIAN ACCORDING TO THE ERA OF 61 C.E.

66. Æ medium bronze. 87 C.E. 6.40 gr. 20/21 mm.

Obverse:
Laureate head of Domitian to right. Border of dots.
Legend, around from lower left: IM(perator) CA(esar) D(ivi) VES(pasiani) F(ilius) D[O]M(itianus) A[V(gustus) G]ER(manicus) CO(n)S(ul) XII (Emperor Caesar, son of divine Vespasian, Domitian Augustus Germanicus, Consul for the twelfth time).

Reverse:
Double cornucopia; within, winged caduceus. Border of dots.
Legend, around from left: ΕΠΙ ΒΑ ΑΓΡ (By King Agrippa); in field flanking: ET KS (26th year [of the reign of Agrippa II, 87 C.E.]); below: S(enatus) C(onsulto) [= by the decree of the Senate].

Bibliography: *Narkiss*, No. 68; *Reifenberg*, No. 106; *Meshorer*, No. 143; *Hill*, pp. 245–246, Nos. 49–50.

67. Æ medium bronze. 87 C.E. 4.65 gr. 19/20 mm.

Obverse:
Laureate head of Domitian to right. Border of dots.
Legend, around from left below: [IM] CA[D VE]S F DOM AV GER COS XII (see No. 66).

Reverse:
Border of dots. Dot in center.
Legend, in center: S C (in large letters); in semi-circle upward from left to right: ΕΠΙ ΒΑ ΑΓΡΙ; below: ET KS (26th year [of Agrippa's reign, 87 C.E.]).

Bibliography: *Narkiss*, No. 69; *Reifenberg*, No. 105; *Meshorer*, No. 142; *Hill*, p. 246. No. 51.

no. 67

WITHOUT IMPERIAL PORTRAIT, ERA BEGINNING 56 C.E.

68. Æ minor bronze. 91 C.E. 1.50 gr. 13/14 mm.

Obverse:
Male head (Agrippa II?) to right, turreted. Border of dots.
Legend, around on right: ΒΑ ΑΓΡ (King Agrippa).

Reverse:
Cornucopia. Border of dots.
Legend, flanking: ΕΤ ΔΛ̄ (34th year [of Agrippa's reign, 91 C.E.]).
There is an interesting parallel between the obverse here (on which a turreted male head is depicted) and a denarius issued in 13 B.C.E. by Augustus, with Marcus Agrippa, Augustus' general, on the reverse. This may represent a copy of the denarius, especially since Agrippa II's full name in Latin was Marcus Julius Agrippa, like that of the Roman general (see H. Mattingly and E. A. Sydenham, *The Roman Imperial Coinage*, I, London, 1923, p. 77, No. 172).

Bibliography: *Reifenberg*, No. 117; *Meshorer*, No. 145; *Hill*, p. 247, Nos. 63–64.

V. THE JEWISH WAR AGAINST ROME (66–70 C.E.).

The dissatisfaction of the people during the period of Roman procuratorial rule in Judea led from time to time to outbreaks and bloodshed – and to their suppression by the Roman legions. The riots which broke out at Caesarea in 66 C.E. were very serious. Though suffering heavy losses, the Jews gained the upper hand and the Roman occupation forces were driven out of most of the country, encouraging the great majority of the population to oppose the Roman army openly. Until the destruction of the Second Temple in 70 C.E., a bitter war was waged between the Jewish inhabitants of the country and the Roman legions, with the latter slowly regaining the positions they had lost at the beginning of the revolt. The war broke out under Nero, and the general sent by him to quell it was Vespasian. The city of Acre-Ptolemais served as a bridgehead, and he first reconquered the northern part of the country – Galilee. Here he captured the Jewish area commander, Josephus Flavius, who became the greatest Jewish historian of the period and of the war. In 69 C.E., Jerusalem was besieged and, on the Ninth of Av, 70 C.E., the Temple was destroyed. By this time, Vespasian had already become emperor at Rome, and the command of the legions in Eretz Israel devolved upon his son, Titus. According to Josephus, who lived in the Roman camp as a favorite of the Romans during those fateful days, the Roman high command decided not to touch the Temple, but soldiers took the matter into their own hands and put it to the torch. Tens of thousands of Jews were killed during the fighting and, when the Temple fell, aspirations for Jewish independence faded for generations.

During the war, the Jews gave expression to their independence and freedom from Rome not only by striking bronze coins, but also by issuing silver coinage – an act which, within the framework of the Roman Empire, was the sole privilege of the emperor. These coins are the thick shekels, half-shekels, and quarter-shekels, famous for their simple beauty and fine artistic execution, issued in the name of "Jerusalem the Holy." They are dated according to the era of the war, from "Year one" to "Year five," but remain anonymous, not bearing the names of the leaders of the revolt. The shekels of the fifth year are very rare, for only three months of that year passed before the final catastrophe and it is unlikely that many were minted during the turmoil of the siege. The bronze coins issued during this fateful period, also anonymous, bear legends and slogans of the war, such as "Freedom of Zion" and "Redemption of Zion." The patterns on the coins of the first Jewish War were borrowed from contemporary Jewish art, motifs which are repeated at a later period in the synagogue art of Eretz Israel in the Talmudic period: the chalice and amphora, and floral patterns such as three pomegranates, a vine-leaf, a palm-tree, the *lulav*, and the *etrog*.

no. 74

ISSUES OF THE FIRST YEAR

69. Æ shekel. 66/67 C.E. 14.10 gr. 22/23 mm.

Obverse:
Branch with three fruits (unripe pomegranates?). Border of dots.
Legend, around from lower right: ⊒ש⊲ר⊅ ⅃⅃ש⊳⅁ר⊥ ירושלם קדשה
(Jerusalem the Holy).

Reverse:
Chalice on high stem with knop; two pearls beneath rim. Border of dots.
Legend, around from lower right: ⅃ₓₒ⊳ש⊤ ⅃⊲⊳ש שקל ישראל (Shekel of
Israel); in field above chalice: ⊤ א (1st [year of the Jewish War, 66/67 C.E.]).

Bibliography: *Narkiss*, No. 74; *Reifenberg*, No. 137; *Meshorer*, No. 148; *Hill*, p. 269, Nos.
1–4; Kadman, Jewish War, No. 2.

70. Æ half-shekel. 66/67 C.E. 6.50 gr. 20 mm.

Obverse:
Branch with three fruits (unripe pomegranates?). Border of dots.
Legend, around from lower right: ⊒ש⊲ר⊅ ⅃⅃ש⊳⅁ר⊥ ירושלם קדשה
(Jerusalem the Holy).

Reverse:
Chalice on high stem with knop; two pearls beneath rim. Border of dots.
Legend, around from lower right: ⅃ ⊤שₓ ₓₘ ⊟ חצי השקל (Half-
shekel); in field above chalice: ⊤ א (1st [year of the Jewish War, 66/67 C.E.]).

Bibliography: *Narkiss*, No. 76; *Reifenberg*, No. 138; *Meshorer*, No. 149; *Hill*, p. 269, Nos.
5–6; Kadman, *Jewish War*, No. 4.

ISSUES OF THE SECOND YEAR

71. Æ shekel. 67/68 C.E. 14.20 gr. 22 mm.

Obverse:

Branch with three fruits (unripe pomegranates?). Border of dots.
Legend, around from lower right: ⲋⲱⳋⳕⳔⳅ⳺Ⳕⲗⲗⲱⳕⳕⳝ ירושלים הקדושה
(Jerusalem the Holy).

Reverse:

Chalice on high stem with knop; nine pearls on rim. Border of dots.
Legend, around from lower right: ⳶ⳛⳕⲱⲗ ⳶ⳝⲱ שקל ישראל
(Shekel of Israel); in field above chalice ⳾ⲱ ב(נת)ש (2nd year [of the Jewish War, 67/68 C.E.]).

Bibliography: *Narkiss*, No. 75; *Reifenberg*, No. 139; *Meshorer*, No. 151; *Hill*, p. 270, Nos. 7–9; Kadman, *Jewish War*, No. 7.

72. Æ half-shekel. 67/68 C.E. 6.05 gr. 18/19 mm.

Obverse:

Branch with three fruits (unripe pomegranates?). Border of dots.
Legend, around from lower right: ⲋⲱⳋⳕⳔⳅ⳺ⲗⲗⲱⳕⳕⳝ ירושלם קדשה
(Jerusalem the Holy).

Reverse:

Chalice on high stem with knop; seven pearls on rim. Border of dots.
Legend, around from lower right: ⳶ⳕⲱⳋⳕⳅⲱ ⲇ חצי השקל (Half-shekel); in field, above chalice: ⳾ⲱ ב (נת)ש (2nd year [of the Jewish War, 67/68 C.E.]).

Bibliography: *Narkiss*, No. 77; *Reifenberg*, No. 140; *Meshorer*, No. 152; *Hill*, p. 270, Nos. 10–11; Kadman, *Jewish War*, No. 9.

73. Æ perutah. 67/68 C.E. 3.60 gr. 17/21 mm.

Obverse:

Vine-branch with single leaf and tendril. Border of dots.
Legend, around from upper left: [ⳋⳕⳅ]ⲙ ⲭⳕⲇ חרות ציון
(The Freedom of Zion).

Reverse:

Amphora with ribbed body, on stem with knop. Border of dots.
Legend, around from upper left: ⳋ⳻ⲭⲱ ⲭⳋⲱ שנת שתים
(2nd year [of the Jewish War, 67/68 C.E.]).

Bibliography: *Narkiss*, No. 79; *Reifenberg*, No. 147; *Meshorer*, No. 153; *Hill*, p. 273, Nos. 34–40; Kadman, *Jewish War*, No. 14.

ISSUES OF THE THIRD YEAR

74. Æ shekel. 68/69 C.E. 14.30 gr. 21/22 mm.

Obverse:
Branch with three fruits (unripe pomegranates?). Border of dots.
Legend, around from lower right: ⅎWϓ⅄ϘⅎℲℲℳⵏℓWϓ⅁ℳ ירושלים הקדושה
(Jerusalem the Holy).

Reverse:
Chalice on high stem with knop; nine pearls on rim. Border of dots.
Legend, around from lower right: ℓℲℍWⵏ ℓϘW שקל ישראל (Shekel
of Israel); in field above chalice: ℸ W ג (נת)ש (3rd year [of the Jewish War,
68/69 C.E.]).

Bibliography: *Narkiss*, No. 75; *Reifenberg*, No. 141; *Meshorer*, No. 154; *Hill*, p. 270, Nos.
12–14; Kadman, *Jewish War*, No. 20.

75. Æ half-shekel. 68/69 C.E. 6.95 gr. 17 mm.

Obverse:
Branch with three fruits (unripe pomegranates?). Border of dots.
Legend, around from lower right: ⅎWϓ⅄ϓℲℳⵏℓWϓ⅁ℳ ירושלים הקדושה
(Jerusalem the Holy).

Reverse:
Chalice on high stem with knop; seven dots on rim. Border of dots.
Legend, around from lower right: ℓ┬WℲⵏℳ ⊟ חצי השקל (Half-
shekel); in field, above chalice: ℸ W ג (נת)ש (3rd year [of the Jewish War,
68/69 C.E.]).

Bibliography: *Narkiss*, No. 77; *Reifenberg*, No. 142; *Meshorer*, No. 155; *Hill*, p. 271, Nos.
15–16; Kadman, *Jewish War*, No. 23.

76. Æ perutah. 68/69 C.E. 2.70 gr. 17/18 mm.

Obverse:
Vine-branch with single leaf and tendril. Border of dots.
Legend, around from upper left: ℈ϓℲℳ ⵏℸϓ⅁[⊟] חרות ציון
(The Freedom of Zion).

Reverse:
Amphora with ribbed body, narrow neck and two handles, on stem with
knop, ribbed cover with dot finial and dotted rim. Border of dots.
Legend, around from upper left: WϓℓW ⵏ℈W שנת שלוש (3rd year
[of the Jewish War, 68/69 C.E.]).

Bibliography: *Narkiss*, No. 80; *Reifenberg*, No. 148; *Meshorer*, No. 156; *Hill*, pp. 274–275,
Nos. 42–53; Kadman, *Jewish War*, No. 24.

ISSUES OF THE FOURTH YEAR

77. Æℝ shekel. 69/70 C.E. 13.70 gr. 20/21 mm.

Obverse:

Branch with three fruits (unripe pomegranates ?). Border of dots.
Legend, around from lower right: ⟨hebrew⟩ ירושלים הקדושה
(Jerusalem the Holy).

Reverse:

Chalice on high stem with knop; nine pearls on rim. Border of dots.
Legend, around from lower right: ⟨hebrew⟩ שקל ישראל (Shekel
of Israel); in field above chalice: ⟨hebrew⟩ שנת ד' (4th year [of the Jewish War,
69/70 C.E.]).

Bibliography: *Narkiss*, No. 75; *Reifenberg*, No. 143; *Meshorer*, No. 158; *Hill*, p. 271, Nos.
17–18; Kadman, *Jewish War*, No. 27.

78. Æ quarter-shekel (?). 69/70 C.E. 8.10 gr. 23 mm.

Obverse:

Etrog with knop at top. Border of dots.
Legend, around from upper left: ⟨hebrew⟩ לגאלת ציון
(Of the Redemption of Zion).

Reverse:

Two upright *lulavim*. Border of dots.
Legend, around in three quarter circle leftward from right above:
⟨hebrew⟩ שנת ארבע רביע (4th year [of the Jewish War, 69/70
C.E.]; Quarter [shekel ?]).

Bibliography: *Narkiss*, No. 2; *Reifenberg*, No. 5; *Meshorer*, No. 162; *Hill*, pp. 184–185,
Nos. 4–9; Kadman, *Jewish War*, No. 33.

79. Æ eighth-shekel (?). 69/70 C.E. 6.85 gr. 20 mm.

Obverse:

Chalice on high stem with knop; nine pearls on rim. Border of dots.
Legend, around from lower right: ⟨hebrew⟩ לגאלת ציון
(Of the Redemption of Zion).

Reverse:

Lulav flanked by two *etrogim* with knops at top. Border of dots.
Legend, in semi-circle upward from right to left: ⟨hebrew⟩ שנת ארבע
(4th year [of the Jewish War, 69/70 C.E.]).

Bibliography: *Narkiss*, No. 3; *Reifenberg*, No. 6; *Meshorer*, No. 163; *Hill*, pp. 185–187,
Nos. 10–37; Kadman, *Jewish War*, No. 37.

ISSUE OF THE FIFTH YEAR

80. Æ shekel. 70 C.E. 13.00 gr. 21 mm.

Obverse:
Branch with three fruits (unripe pomegranates ?). Border of dots.
Legend, around from lower right: ⌐ꟿ꙯ꙮꝑꟿꟾꟁ⟋ꟽꙮꟿꙮꟁ ירושלים הקדושה
(Jerusalem the Holy).

Reverse:
Chalice on high stem with knop; nine pearls on rim. Border of dots.
Legend, around from lower right: ⟋ꟻꟃꟽꟁ ⟋Ꝓꟽ שקל ישראל (Shekel of
Israel); in field above chalice: ⌐ꟽ׳ה ש(נת) (5th year [of the Jewish War,
70 C.E.]).

Bibliography: *Narkiss*, No. 75; *Reifenberg*, No. 145; *Meshorer*, No. 164; *Hill*, p. 271, No. 20;
Kadman, *Jewish War*, No. 45.

no. 80

VI. THE BAR KOKHBA REVOLT (132–135 C.E.)

Sixty-two years after the destruction of the Second Temple, the second major war against the Romans broke out – the Bar Kokhba Revolt. Carefully and secretly prepared, this war was prompted by Hadrian's wish to instill Greco-Roman culture with still greater force, by prohibiting circumcision and erecting a temple to Jupiter Capitolinus on the Temple Mount. The spiritual leader of the revolt was Rabbi Akiva, while the military and civil leader was Simeon Bar Koseva ("Bar Kokhba"). This war was much more fierce than the first Jewish revolt and the Romans were initially hard pressed. The Twenty-second Legion was defeated and completely wiped out and Hadrian, in his report to the Senate at the end of the war, omitted the customary mention of his own health and of the army's well-being.

The exact extent of the territory controlled by Bar Kokhba is not quite clear, but he certainly held the Hebron district, part of Idumea, and the Dead Sea region (where the last of his fighters took shelter in the desert caves). It is not known for certain whether he indeed took Jerusalem, if only for a short time. The last major stand was at Bethar, and the war came to an end following Bar Kokhba's death there.

Hadrian was now free to proceed with his plans for the paganization of Jerusalem, changing the name of the city to Aelia Capitolina. Jews were forbidden even to enter the new city under pain of death.

From his coins, and from documents found in the Judean desert, it is known that Bar Kokhba styled himself "*Nasi* [Prince] of Israel." The "Bar Kokhba" form of his name stems not from Jewish, but from Christian sources. Until the discovery of the Judean Desert cave material, this name was related to Rabbi Akiva's saying, "a star out of Jacob," and the form "Bar-Kozivah" ("Son of Deceit") was regarded as a derogatory appellation given after his defeat, since he was then regarded as a false Messiah. The coins of this revolt constitute the last ancient Jewish coinage and it is quite remarkable that, in that hour of bitter struggle and dire peril, the Jews took pains to mint the most pleasing series of coins issued in this country. Three authorities appear on these coins: (a) "Jerusalem"; (b) "Simeon (Ben-Koseva), Prince of Israel"; and (c) "Eleazar the Priest." The identity of Eleazar is unknown, but it has been suggested that he was Bar Kokhba's maternal uncle and may have been the high priest designate in anticipation of the Temple cult's restoration.

Bar Kokhba learned much from the Romans, not only in the military sphere but also in civil administration. This is fully revealed in the documents from the Judean Desert caves. Those lands which had been confiscated in this country by Vespasian at the end of the First Jewish War, and which had thus become Imperial estates, later leased to local inhabitants, passed as an inheritance from emperor to emperor, and were in turn confiscated by Bar Kokhba and leased in his own name, as head of the Jewish state, to local Jewish farmers. Among the documents from the caves are abstracts from the district records witnessing such transactions. Bar Kokhba also learned from the Romans how to utilize coinage as a means of mass propaganda; hence the nationalistic motifs and slogans that appear on these coins.

Unlike regular authorities, Bar Kokhba did not strike coins on cast flans, but rather utilized current Roman coinage, restriking new patterns over the older Roman designs – tetradrachms, drachms, and denarii, all current in Eretz Israel at that period, as well as the various bronze values, especially coins of Ashkelon and Gaza. The coins are dated by the era of the war, and the wording used changed from year to year (though in the documents from the caves it remains constant). On the coins we read: "Year One of the Redemption of Israel" (and in documents even "Year Four of the Redemption of Israel"); the next year the date reads: "Y(ear) Two of the Free(dom) of Israel"; while in the third year we find: "For the Freedom of Jerusalem." During this war the name "Israel" replaced the "Zion" of the first Jewish Revolt in both coins and documents.

The motifs of the Bar Kokhba coins are decidedly Jewish and are mostly drawn from the same traditional repertoire as that used in the earlier war; they are connected in the main with the service of the Temple and depict the Temple façade, the musical instruments that accompanied the Levites during worship (two types of lyre, and trumpets), an oil juglet, and an amphora. There are also several floral motifs, some connected with worship – the *lulav* and *etrog*, a palm branch, a bunch of grapes, and a wreath of leaves.

The denominations issued in this series are necessarily the same as those current in the land prior to the war: the silver tetradrachm (*sela* in the Mishnah), denarius (the Mishnaic *zuz*), and four sizes of bronze coins whose original names are unidentified and are thus today denoted as "large," "medium A," "medium B," and "small" bronzes.

The plethora of motifs led to numerous types, and often we also find hybrid types, that is, coins bearing a combination of dies that do not accord with the general issues known to us.

In attempting to ascertain the order in which Bar Kokhba's coins were issued, early scholars sought to use the form of legend as a criterion: (a) "For the Freedom of Jerusalem"; (b) "Year One of the Redemption of Israel"; and (c) "Y(ear) Two of the Free(dom) of Israel." It was originally assumed that the initial legend (a), the slogan: "For the Freedom of Jerusalem," was superseded when its aim was achieved in the first year of the war, and that subsequently Bar Kokhba was able to change the era of the war to "Year One of the Redemption of Israel" in the following year. Thus, "Year One" was issued in the second year of the war, and the coins of legend (c) were issued in the third year. However, both the coins and the documents from the Judean Desert prove just the opposite, i.e., that the undated coins (a) are the last in the series and were thus issued in the third year of the war (134/135 C.E.), as we have classified them below.

The Bar Kokhba series of coins includes numerous die types which were used in various combinations, making it reasonably possible to unravel the chronological order of their issue during the war. The chronological classification of the series is based on a graphical reconstruction of the order in which the Bar Kokhba coins were struck in the light of the fact that the same dies were used for various coins of different years, and that various types of dies were used.

The side bearing the name of the issuing authority – "Shim'on" (Simeon), "Eleazar the Priest," or "Jerusalem" – is to be regarded as the obverse.

(a) *First year:* "Jerusalem" around in three-quarter circle from right to left upward; Temple façade (*shin* form always rounded: ω).

(b) *Second year:* "Shim'on" (Bar Kokhba's name) – during the first half of the year only part of the name, שמע in two lines on the denarii and in one line on the medium bronze A (*shin* [ω] still always rounded); in the second half of the year, the name in full on the tetradrachms and medium bronze A, and in corrupt form on the denarii (the *shin* form is always angular: W). The coins of the second half of the year are also characterized by the form of the last two letters of the name: ל ח.

(c) *Third year:* The last two letters of "Shim'on" consistently appear as: ל א. Each denomination has a die-combination of its own, except for the denarii No. 94 and Nos. 89, 90, and 91, and the small bronzes (of Eleazar the Priest), for which the same dies were used: the cluster of grapes with "Year One of the Redemption of Israel" (these are entirely different denominations, though of similar diameter). The diagrams below demonstrate the chronological order of the various Bar Kokhba coins on the basis of the die-combinations, each denomination separately.

1. TETRADRACHMS

(A) The sequence from Year One to Year Two (133 C.E.): The die with the name "Jerusalem" divided into three groups of two letters in three-quarter circle around the Temple façade was used in the first and second years: ‏יר־וש־לם‏ (2)* Here the use of the round ‏ω‏ is characteristic. The rarity of this die's appearance in the second year in conjunction with the second year's die (3), indicates that it was probably used then only during the early part of that year (133 C.E.). During the first half of the second year, the name "Jerusalem" as minting authority was still retained, but a new die was used (4), on which the name was divided into two groups of letters, as was later the name "Shim῾on". In the second half of the second year, the tetradrachms bear the name "Shim῾on" instead of "Jerusalem," the final two letters of the name appearing in the form: ‏ זﬡ‏ (6); the *shin* form is angular ‏W‏ on the reverse (5). This type was undoubtedly issued in the second half of the second year.

(B) The sequence from the second year to the third year (134 C.E.): As early as the beginning of the third year, the last two letters of the name "Shim῾on" appear as ‏ זﬡ‏ (7). Coin No. 98 is an example of the second year reverse die's continued appearance at the start of the third year.

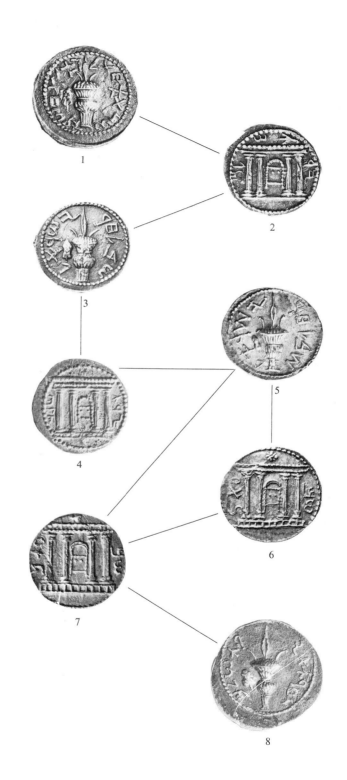

* Henceforth numbers in parentheses refer to the respective diagrams.

2. DENARII

The abundance of the die combinations on the denarii enables us to determine which dies were used at the beginning of a given year, whether in the first or the second half of the year. The diagram illustrates the chronological sequence revealed by a study of these dies; the common die-types are as follows:

(A) Dies bearing the name of the issuing authority:
  1. Eleazar the Priest – juglet with palm branch.
  2. Shim'on (with variants) שמע, שמעונ, שמנעו – within wreath.
  3. Shim'on – bunch of grapes.
(B) Dies bearing dates:
  1. Year One of the Redemption of Israel – bunch of grapes.
  2. Y(ear) Two of the Free(dom) of Israel – wide lyre.
  3. Y(ear) Two of the Free(dom) of Israel; or: For the Freedom of Jerusalem – palm branch.
  4. Y(ear) Two of the Free(dom) of Israel; or: For the Freedom of Jerusalem – juglet with small palm branch.
  5. Y(ear) Two of the Free(dom) of Israel; or: For the Freedom of Jerusalem – two trumpets.
  6. Y(ear) Two of the Free(dom) of Israel; or: For the Freedom of Jerusalem – elongated lyre.
  7. For the Freedom of Jerusalem – juglet (without palm branch).

(A) DENARIUS OF YEAR ONE (132 C.E.)

There is only one type of denarius bearing this date. It was struck in the name of Eleazar the Priest and only three examples are known. The best preserved copy is in the Vatican Museum in Rome (1–2 in the diagram). The reverse die (bunch of grapes) of the first year (1) was, however, used extensively for the minting of small bronze coins of "Eleazar the Priest" (3) and scarcely at all for "Jerusalem" (4). Since most of the coins struck from this die of the first year are of bronze, we are left with the impression that its use for the silver denarii was accidental, especially since – as we will see below – this same die appears on other hybrid types, in conjunction with dies of the second year (5, 6). Other such hybrids are formed with the obverse of Eleazar the Priest (2) and early obverses of the second year bearing the name "Shim'on" (7).

(B) EARLY SECOND YEAR (133 C.E.)

The die with a bunch of grapes and the legend "Year One of the Redemption of Israel" (1) appears with the die of the second year with the broad lyre (6) or with the palm branch (5), in both cases with the rounded form of the letter *shin*. It would seem that the wreath surrounding the abbreviated name

(A) First Year (132/133 C.E.)

(B) Early Second Year
(133 C.E.)

(C) First Half of Second Year
(133 C.E.)

(D) Second Half of Second Year
(134 C.E.)

(E) Beginning of Third Year
(134 C.E.)

(F) Third Year up to End of War
(134/135 C.E.)

of Shim'on (7) was already in use at the time. This die appears initially in conjunction with the die of Eleazar the Priest, with juglet and small branch (2), from the first year, and with the two dies mentioned above – the wide lyre (6) and the palm branch (5) with rounded *shin* (ɯ).

(C) FIRST HALF OF THE SECOND YEAR (133 C.E.)

At this time, the die with the abbreviated name "Shim'on" in a wreath (7) is used in conjunction with new dies, such as the jug with branch (8) and the two trumpets (9), both with angular *shin* (w); even in the name "Shim'on" the form of the *shin* is angular. Apparently parallel to this, another new die was brought into use, featuring a cluster of grapes and the name "Shim'on," the last two letters of which have the form: ﬩ (11). This die appears with the wide lyre (6) and the palm branch (5) with rounded *shin* (ɯ), as well as the palm branch with angular *shin* (w). (10)

(D) SECOND HALF OF SECOND YEAR (134 C.E.)

In addition to the palm branch with angular *shin* (10), the cluster of grapes (11) now also appears with the elongated lyre and angular *shin* (12). Furthermore, a new die comes into use – the wreath enclosing a corrupt form of the name "Shim'on", with letters typical of the second year in their form: (13). This die occurs here together with the palm branch and rounded *shin* (5) as well as with the elongated lyre (12), the palm branch (10), and the juglet with palm branch (8), all with angular *shin*.

(E) BEGINNING OF THIRD YEAR (134 C.E.)

At the start of this year, the wreath enclosing the name "Shim'on" in a corrupt form – the die of the second half of the second year (13) – now appears with the following third year dies: juglet with small palm branch (19), elongated lyre (21), two trumpets (22), and palm branch (23), as well as with the palm branch with its tip bent to the left (15), the latter apparently from the beginning of the year. The cluster of grapes (first half of the second year – 11) and the palm branch of the third year (23) also appear to have been struck at this time. In this same year, a new type of die was introduced, bearing the cluster of grapes with the name "Shim'on" שמעון, the *shin* still being angular (16). In the British Museum, there is one copy of this coin combining the cluster of grapes with the palm branch (23) of the third year.

(F) THIRD YEAR UP TO THE END OF THE WAR (134/135 C.E.)

Of this period no less than 15 types are known. These include three groups of obverse, such as the cluster of grapes mentioned above (24) and the wreath enclosing two spellings of the name "Shim'on" (both corrupt) with five reverse types – the juglet with palm branch (19), juglet without palm branch (20), elongated lyre (21), two trumpets (22), and palm branch (23). The unique combination of the wreath enclosing the corrupt "Shim'on" (18) and the wide lyre with rounded *shin* (6) of the second year is of interest. Such combinations of chronologically "distant" dies will also be encountered in dealing with the bronze coins of Bar Kokhba. As we have seen, there are no denarii of the first year bearing the name of "Shim'on" (Bar Kokhba). As from the second year, however, an abbreviated form of this name becomes quite typical (7), appearing on the medium bronze A (see 3 *ibid*. below) as well. As on the tetradrachms (6 *ibid*.) and the bronze coins (5), we find on the denarii (11, 13) the last two letters of the name "Shim'on" in the second half of the second year occurring in a typical form: ʃ ħ. This leads one to the assumption that those denarii of the third year which still bear this form of script date from the very beginning of the year, when the dies of the previous year were still usable.

The denarii of the third year bear the name of "Shim'on" with the last two letters in the form: ʒ ⅄ (16, 17, 18, 24), as on the other values. During the two last years of the war, two parallel series were actually issued, bearing the wreath on the obverse (7, 13, 17, and 18) or the bunch of grapes (11, 16, and 24), both types with the name "Shim'on." The reverse bears the date in various forms, such as the juglet with small palm branch (8, 19), juglet alone (20), wide lyre (6), elongated lyre (12, 14, 21), two trumpets (9, 22), or the palm branch (5, 10, 15, 23), but only in the third year are all possible combinations of the dies to be found.

The motif of the juglet with palm branch passed from the obverse (on the coins of "Eleazar the Priest" – (2) to the reverse, as from the second half of the second year (8), and later (19). The palm branch is bent to the left in the second year (10) and to the right in the third year (23), except in one example where it inclines to the left (15), possibly indicating that it dates from the beginning of that year. Two similar cases are those of a still angular *shin* (in the name "Shim'on") with a cluster of grapes, associated with third year-type final letters: ʒ ⅄ (16), and of an elongated lyre, still small, like that of the second year, which appears at the beginning of the third year (14).

The juglet without palm branch appears only in the third year (20). It would thus seem that the hybrid denarii in which dies of the first and second years were used, and those with dies of the second and third years, provide us with the links for a reconstruction of the sequence from year to year.

3. LARGE BRONZE

The die featuring "Jeru/salem" ירו שלם within a wreath (No. 82) was in use during the first and second years (probably only in the first half of the second year).

4. MEDIUM BRONZE A

The pattern for this denomination is uniform: a palm-tree with the name "Shim´on" (1, 3, 5, 7), together with a vine-leaf and the date on the reverse (2, 4, 6, 8). This is the most common denomination among coins of the Bar Kokhba war, and hence the plurality of dies. It is readily possible, however, to distinguish the different dies and to fix the time of their appearance and the sequence from year to year. It should be noted here that the full formula, "Shim´on *Nasi* of Israel" שמעון נשיא ישראל (1), appears only on bronze coins of the first year; there are no silver coins from the first year bearing his name.

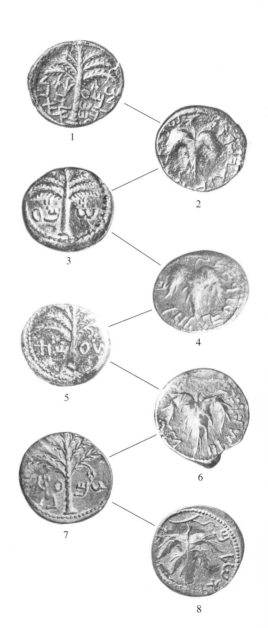

(A) FIRST YEAR (132/133 C.E.)

Flanking a palm-tree: "Shim'on *Nasi* of Israel" (1) around vine-leaf: "Year One of the Redemption of Israel" (2).

(B) BEGINNING OF THE SECOND YEAR (133 C.E.)

Flanking a palm-tree: the abbreviation "Shim'[on]" (שמע) (3), instead of "Shim'on *Nasi* of Israel", the same abbreviation appearing in the first half of the second year on the denarii (see *ibid.*, above 7); the die with the vine-leaf from the first year was still in use (2), and so this combination was probably used only at the beginning of the second year, despite the fact that the first year inscription appears. Coins of this combination are quite rare.

(C) FIRST HALF OF SECOND YEAR (133 C.E.)

Flanking a palm-tree, the abbreviated form of "Shim'on" (שמע) (3), linked with the die of the vine-leaf and the date of the second year of the war (4), with a rounded *shin* ω.

(D) SECOND HALF OF SECOND YEAR (134 C.E.)

Flanking a palm-tree, "Shim'on" in full, the last two letters in the form: ן) ל ħ) typical of silver coins of this same phase; on the side of the vine-leaf (6) the *shin* is angular (w).

(E) BEGINNING OF THIRD YEAR (134 C.E.)

Coin No. 114 is a typical example of the use of dies in the transition from one year to the next. The date of the second year still appears around the vine-leaf(6), with angular *shin*, as the die was still usable; on the obverse, however, the palm-tree is flanked by the name "Shim'on," the last two letters of which display the form appearing only in the third year: ן) ל א (7).

(F) THIRD YEAR UNTIL THE END OF THE WAR (134/135 C.E.)

Flanking a palm-tree, we find script typical of the first half of the year (7), and around the vine-leaf appears the legend: "For the Freedom of Jerusalem" (8).

5. MEDIUM BRONZE B

This value is generally uniform in its motifs, although it differs in the third year. In the first and second years there is a wreath enclosing a palm branch, the whole surrounded by the legend: "שמעון נשיא ישראל"—"Shimʿon *Nasi* of Israel" (2); on the reverse is a wide lyre and the appropriate date (1, 3).

(A) FIRST YEAR (132/133 C.E.)

On the obverse, a wreath enclosing an upright palm branch; around: "Shimʿon *Nasi* of Israel" (2); on the reverse, a wide lyre, around which is the date: "שנת אחת לגאלת ישראל" —"Year One of the Redemption of Israel" (1).

(B) SECOND YEAR (133/134 C.E.)

As in the first year, but around the lyre is the legend: "Y(ear) 2 of the Free(dom) of Israel" (3), with either rounded [ω] or angular *shin* [W]. According to the practice demonstrated above regarding the denarii, the rounded form was mainly common during the first half of the second year, whereas the angular form was more common during the second half of the year.

(C) BEGINNING OF THIRD YEAR (134 C.E.)

Hybrid coin. On the one side is the wide lyre with "ש״ב׳ לחר׳ ישראל"—"Y(ear) 2 of the Free(dom) of Israel" (3), with either rounded or angular *shin*; on the other side, a wreath enclosing an upright palm branch, with the surrounding legend: "לחרות ירושלם" —"For the Freedom of Jerusalem" (4).

(D) THIRD YEAR UNTIL THE END OF THE WAR (134/135 C.E.)

Obverse: elongated lyre; around: "שמעון"—"Shimʿon" (5); reverse: wreath enclosing upright palm branch, with the surrounding legend: "לחרות ירושלם" —"For the Freedom of Jerusalem" (4).

The hybrid coin of the beginning of the third year provides the link in the sequence of coins from the second year to the third, and is thus one of the most important examples that support the theory that the slogan "For the Freedom of Jerusalem" was struck in the third year, and not in the first.

6. SMALL BRONZE

The small bronze coins are uniform, i.e., the obverse shows a palm-tree flanked by the name of the issuing authority, such as "Eleazar the Priest" (1) or "Jerusalem" (5, 6) in the first and second years, and "Shim'on" (7) as well in the third year. On the reverse, they display a cluster of grapes with the appropriate date around (2–4). The diagram shows the sequence of dies and indicates that the same dies were used for the obverse of the types with the name of Eleazar in the first year (1) and the coins of the second and third years. The coins of the second year bearing his name are, however, uncommon, while those of the third year bearing his name are extremely rare. A problem arises as to whether these issues in the name of Eleazar the Priest of the second (1 + 4) and third (1 + 3) years are accidental or not, since there are no other denominations from these years bearing his name.

The coins bearing "Jerusalem" as the issuing authority are also quite rare, especially those of the first year (2 + 5). There are at least two different dies, one with the rounded *shin* (5), appearing in conjunction with the die of the first year and apparently used also at the beginning of the second year. The same form of *shin*, known to be the style of the first half of the second year, is also found here in "Jerusalem," in conjunction with the second year die (4 + 5). But the angular form of the *shin* in "Jerusalem" also occurs in conjunction with the second year dies (4 + 6), and it would seem that these coins are to be assigned to the second half of the second year. The angular *shin* appears also on coins of the third year (4 + 6), which seem to have been minted in the first half of that year (134 C.E.). In the legend ‏"שׁ״ב׳ לחר׳ ישראל"‏ on (4), the *shin* is always angular, and in accordance with the form on the other denominations this die must date from the second half of the second year.

There is one additional type, that bearing the name "Shim'on" flanking a palm-tree (7). This appears only in conjunction with the die of the third year (3 + 7) and therefore poses no chronological problem.

In the above, we have seen the sequence of dies from the first to the second, and from the second to the third years. Thus, the accepted chronological order is proven: (A) Year One of the Redemption of Israel (132/133 C.E.); (B) Y(ear) 2 of the Free(dom) of Israel (133/134 C.E.); and (C) For the Freedom of Jerusalem (134/135 C.E.). The die combinations enable us to determine the chronological order of minting, and to establish the various periods of minting, such as the start of the second year, the first and second halves of the second year, the start of the third year, and the third year up to the end of the war. This holds good for all the denominations issued during the war.

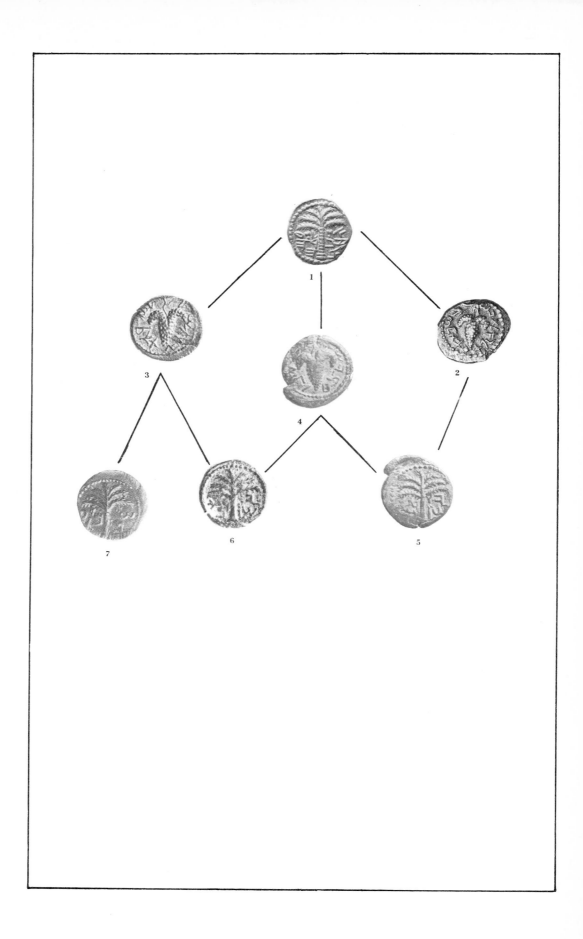

70

ISSUES ENTITLED "JERUSALEM"/"YEAR ONE OF THE REDEMPTION OF ISRAEL"

81. Æ tetradrachm. 132/133 C.E. 14.80 gr. 27/28 mm.

Obverse:
Temple façade: architrave on four ribbed columns with capitals; between two inner columns, Ark (with shelf and scrolls?). Border of dots.
Legend, around from lower right: ⟨glyphs⟩ ירושלם (Jerusalem).

Reverse:
Lulav, with small *etrog* in field on left. Border of dots.
Legend, around from lower right: ⟨glyphs⟩ שנת אחת לגאלת ישראל (Year One of the Redemption of Israel).

Bibliography: *Narkiss*, No. 84; *Reifenberg*, No. 163; *Meshorer*, No. 165; *Hill*, p. 284, No. 1.

82. Æ large bronze. 132/133 C.E. 19.90 gr. 31/33 mm.

Obverse:
Wreath tied at bottom, with leaves in groups of two; above, a kind of medallion closing wreath. Border of dots.
Legend within, in two lines: ⟨glyphs⟩ ירושלם (Jerusalem).

Reverse:
Large amphora with ribbed body, two handles, and high base. Border of dots.
Legend, around from lower right: ⟨glyphs⟩ שנת אחת לגאלת ישראל (Year One of the Redemption of Israel).

Bibliography: *Narkiss*, No. 85; *Reifenberg*, No. 191; *Meshorer*, No. 168; *Hill*, p. 303, No. 9.

83. Æ small bronze (on relatively large flan). 132/133 C.E. 5.20 gr. 20 mm.

Obverse:
Palm-tree with seven branches and two bunches of dates. Border of dots.
Legend, flanking in two lines: ⟨glyphs⟩ ירו [של]ם (Jerusalem).

Reverse:
Cluster of grapes (crude execution). Border of dots.
Legend, around from lower left: ⟨glyphs⟩ שנת אחת לגאלת ישר[אל] (Year One of the Redemption of Isra[el]).

Bibliography: *Narkiss*, No. 86; *Reifenberg*, No. 195; *Meshorer*, No. 175.

84. Æ large bronze. 132/133 C.E. 26.30 gr. 28/31 mm.

Obverse:

Wreath tied at bottom, with leaves in groups of six; above, a kind of medallion
closing wreath. Border of dots.
Legend within, in three lines: 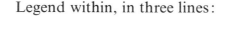 שמעון/נשיא/ישראל
(Shim'on *Nasi* of Israel).

Reverse:

Large amphora with ribbed body, two handles, and high base. Border of dots.
Legend, around from lower right: שנת אחת לגאלת ישראל (Year One of the Redemption of Israel).

Bibliography: *Narkiss*, No. 87; *Reifenberg*, No. 190; *Meshorer*, No. 169; *Hill*, p. 303, Nos.
10–12.

85. Æ large bronze. 132/133 C.E. 22.70 gr. 28/29 mm.

Obverse:

Wreath tied at bottom, with leaves in groups of two; above, a kind of medallion closing wreath. Border of dots.
Legend within, in three lines: שמעון/נשיא/ישראל
(Shim'on *Nasi* of Israel).

Reverse:

Large amphora with ribbed body, two handles, and high base. Border of dots.
Legend, around from lower right: שנת אחת לגאלת ישראל (Year One of the Redemption of Israel).

Bibliography: *Narkiss*, No. 87; *Reifenberg*, No. 190; *Meshorer*, No. 169; *Hill*, p. 304, Nos.
13–14.

no. 81

86. Æ large bronze (on unusually large flan). 132/133 C.E. 45.90 gr. 33/34 mm.

Obverse:

Wreath tied at bottom, with leaves in groups of two; above, a kind of medallion closing wreath. Border of dots.
Legend within, in three lines: שמעון / נשיא / ישראל
(Shim'on *Nasi* of Israel).

Reverse:

Large amphora with ribbed body, two handles, and high base. Border of dots.
Legend, around from lower right: שנת אחת לגאלת ישראל (Year One of the Redemption of Israel).

Bibliography: *Narkiss*, No. 87; *Reifenberg*, No. 190; *Meshorer*, No. 169; *Hill*, p. 304, Nos. 13–14.

87. Æ medium bronze A. 132/133 C.E. 9.85 gr. 23/25 mm.

Obverse:

Palm-tree with seven branches and two bunches of dates. Border of dots.
Legend, in field flanking in four lines: שמעון נשיא ישראל
(Shim'on *Nasi* of Israel).

Reverse:

Vine-leaf hanging from branch. Border of dots.
Legend, around from upper left: שנת אחת לגאלת ישראל (Year One of the Redemption of Israel).

Bibliography: *Narkiss*, No. 89; *Reifenberg*, No. 193; *Meshorer*, No. 170; *Hill*, p. 305, No. 21–25.

88. Æ medium bronze B. 132/133 C.E. 9.80 gr. 21/24 mm.

Obverse:

Wreath tied at bottom, with leaves in groups of three; above, a kind of medallion closing wreath, within, upright palm branch. Border of dots.
Legend, around from lower right: שמעון נשיא ישראל
(Shim'on *Nasi* of Israel).

Reverse:

Broad lyre with five strings. Border of dots.
Legend, around from lower right: שנת אחת לגאלת ישראל (Year One of the Redemption of Israel).

Bibliography: *Narkiss*, No. 88; *Reifenberg*, No. 192; *Meshorer*, No. 172; *Hill*, pp. 304–305, Nos. 15–20.

ISSUES ENTITLED "ELEAZAR THE PRIEST"/"YEAR ONE OF THE REDEMPTION OF ISRAEL"

89. Æ small bronze. 132/133 C.E. 5.50 gr. 17/19 mm.

Obverse:
Palm-tree with seven branches and two bunches of dates. Border of dots. Legend, in field flanking in three lines: 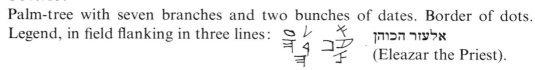 אלעזר הכוהן (Eleazar the Priest).

Reverse:
Bunch of grapes hanging from branch, with small leaf at left. Border of dots. Legend, around from left above: שⁿⁿⁿ שנת אחת לגאלת ישר|אל| (Year One of the Redemption of Isra[el]).

Bibliography: *Narkiss*, No. 91; *Reifenberg*, No. 189; *Meshorer*, No. 173; *Hill*, p. 302, No. 1.

90. Æ small bronze. 132/133 C.E. 8.55 gr. 18/19 mm.

Obverse:
Palm-tree with seven branches and two bunches of dates. Border of dots. Legend, in field flanking in three lines: אלעזר הכוהן (Eleazar the Priest).

Reverse:
Bunch of grapes hanging from branch with small leaf at left. Border of dots. Legend, around from left: שנת אחת לגאלת ישר|אל| (Year One of the Redemption of Isra[el]).

Bibliography: *Narkiss*, No. 91; *Reifenberg*, No. 189; *Meshorer*, No. 173; *Hill*, p. 302, No. 1.

91. Æ small bronze. 132/133 C.E. 5.45 gr. 17/20 mm.

Obverse:
Palm-tree with seven branches and two bunches of dates. Border of dots. Legend, in field flanking in two lines (retrograde): אלעזר הכוהן (Eleazar the Priest).

Reverse:
Bunch of grapes hanging from branch with small leaf at left. Border of dots. Legend, around from left above: שנת אחת לגאלת ישר|אל| (Year One of the Redemption of Isra[el]).

Bibliography: *Narkiss*, No. 91; *Reifenberg*, No. 189A; *Meshorer*, No. 174; *Hill*, p. 302, Nos. 2–8.

HYBRID COINS STRUCK FROM FIRST AND SECOND YEAR DIES

92. Æ **tetradrachm. 133/134 C.E. 14.65 gr. 25 mm.**

Obverse:

Temple façade: architrave on four ribbed columns with capitals; between two inner columns, Ark (with shelf and scrolls ?). Border of dots.
Legend, in three-quarter circle upward from right to left: ⅂⅃ ﬡ ﬦ ﬡ ⅂ᵡ
ירוש לם (Jerusalem) (die identical with obverse of No. 81).

Reverse:

Lulav, with small *etrog* in field on left. Border of dots.
Legend, around from lower left: ⅃ﬡﬡﬡﬡﬡﬡﬡﬡ שׁ(נת) ב לחר(ות) ישראל
(Y[ear] 2 of the Free[dom] of Israel).

Bibliography: *Meshorer,* No. 178; Aktiengesellschaft Leu & Co., *Sale Catalogue,* Zurich, *27.3.56,* p. 42, No. 328.

93. Æ **denarius. 133/134 C.E. 3.10 gr. 19 mm.**

Obverse:

Juglet with ribbed body, stem, and one handle; in field on upper right, small palm branch. Border of dots.
Legend, around from upper left: ﬡﬡﬡﬡﬡﬡﬡﬡ אלעזר הכוהן
(Eleazar the Priest).

Reverse:

Wreath tied at bottom, with almond-shaped leaves; above, a kind of medallion closing wreath. Border of dots.
Legend within, in two lines: ﬡﬡ שמ/ע(ון) (Shim´[on]).

Bibliography: *Reifenberg,* No. 169; *Meshorer,* No. 167; *Hill,* p. 288, Nos. 2–3.

94. Æ **denarius. 133/134 C.E. 3.35 gr. 17 mm.**

Obverse:

Bunch of grapes hanging from branch with small leaf at left. Border of dots.
Legend, around from left above: ﬡﬡﬡﬡﬡﬡﬡﬡﬡ
(שׁנת אחת לגאלת ישר(אל (Year One of the Redemption of Isra[el]).

Reverse:

Upright palm branch with tip bent to left. Border of dots.
Legend, around from lower right: ﬡﬡﬡﬡﬡﬡﬡ שׁ(נת) ב׳ לחר(ות) ישראל
(Y[ear] 2 of the Free[dom] of Israel).

Bibliography: *Narkiss,* No. 92A; *Reifenberg,* No. 171; *Meshorer,* No. 176; *Hill,* p. 289, No. 4.

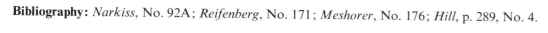

95. Æ **denarius. 132/133 C.E. 3.10 gr. 18/19 mm.**

Obverse:

Bunch of grapes hanging from branch with small leaf at left. Border of dots.
Legend, around from left: שנת אחת לגאלת ישראל
(Year One of the Redemption of Israel).

Reverse:

Broad lyre with three strings. Border of dots.
Legend, in three-quarter circle upward from right below:
(שנת) ב׳ לחר(ות) ישראל   (Y[ear] 2 of the Free[dom] of Israel).

Bibliography: *Narkiss*, No. 92; *Reifenberg*, No. 172; *Meshorer*, No. 177; *Hill*, p. 289, No. 5.

96. Æ **medium bronze A. 133/134 C.E. 11.90 gr. 23/24 mm.**

Obverse:

Palm-tree with seven branches and two bunches of dates. Border of dots.
Legend, in field flanking in one line: ש מע (ון)   (Shim῾[on]).

Reverse:

Vine-leaf hanging on branch. Border of dots.
Legend, around from left above:
שנת אחת לגאלת ישראל   (Year One of the Redemption of Israel).

Bibliography: *Narkiss*, No. 90; *Reifenberg*, No. 194; *Meshorer*, No. 171; *Hill*, p. 306, No. 27.

no. 93

76

ISSUES ENTITLED "SHIM'ON"/"YEAR 2 OF THE FREEDOM OF ISRAEL"

97. Æ tetradrachm. 133/134 C.E. 14.40 gr. 25/26 mm.

Obverse:
Temple façade: architrave on four ribbed columns with capitals, standing on row of ashlars, between two inner columns, Ark (with shelf and scrolls ?). Star above. Border of dots.
Legend, flanking: שמ/עון (Shim'on).

Reverse:
Lulav, with small *etrog* in field on left. Border of dots.
Legend, around from lower right: ש(נת) ב' לחר(ות) ישראל (Y[ear] 2 of the Free[dom] of Israel).

Bibliography: *Narkiss*, No. 94; *Reifenberg*, No. 164; *Meshorer*, No. 181; *Hill*, p. 285, No. 4.

98. Æ tetradrachm. 133/134 C.E. 14/10 gr. 25/26 mm.

Obverse:
Temple façade: architrave on four ribbed columns with capitals, standing on row of ashlars; between two inner columns, Ark (with shelf and scrolls ?). Star above. Border of dots.
Legend, flanking: שמ/עון (Shim'on).

Reverse:
Lulav, with small *etrog* in field on left. Border of dots.
Legend, around from lower right: ש(נת) ב' לחר(ות) ישראל (Y[ear] 2 of the Free[dom] of Israel).

Bibliography: *Narkiss*, No. 94; *Reifenberg*, No. 164; *Meshorer*, No. 181; *Hill*, p. 284, Nos. 2–3.

no. 97

99. Æ denarius. 133/134 C.E. 2.65 gr. 18/20 mm.

Obverse:
Wreath tied below, with almond-shaped leaves; above, a kind of medallion closing wreath. Border of dots.
Legend within, in two lines: ש/ע
Traces of previous striking. שמ/ע(ון) (Shim'[on]).

Reverse:
Juglet with ribbed body, stem, and one handle; in field on upper right, small palm branch. Border of dots.
Legend, around from lower right: שמל[ר]... ישראל ש(נת) ב' לחר(ות) (Y[ear] 2 of the Free[dom] of Israel).

Bibliography: *Narkiss,* No. 96; *Reifenberg,* No. 173; *Meshorer,* No. 183; *Hill,* pp. 289–290, Nos. 6–12.

100. Æ denarius. 133/134 C.E. 3.10 gr. 17/18 mm.

Obverse:
Wreath tied at bottom, with almond-shaped leaves; above, a kind of medallion closing wreath. Dot in center. Border of dots.
Legend within, in two lines: ש/ע שמ/ען (Shim'[on]).

Reverse:
Broad lyre with three strings. Border of dots.
Legend, in three-quarter circle upward from right to left: שמלרש... ש(נת) ב' לחר(ות) ישראל (Y[ear] 2 of the Free[dom] of Israel).

Bibliography: *Meshorer,* No. 186.

101. Æ denarius. 133/134 C.E. 3.10 gr. 18/19 mm.

Obverse:
Wreath tied at bottom, with almond-shaped leaves; above, a kind of medallion closing wreath. Border of dots.
Legend within, in two lines: ש/ע שמ/ע(ון) (Shim'[on]).

Reverse:
Two trumpets with mouthpieces at bottom. Dot in center. Border of dots.
Legend, around from lower right: שמל[ר]... ישראל ש(נת) ב' לחר(ות) (Y[ear] 2 of the Free[dom] of Israel). Vague traces of previous striking.

Bibliography: *Narkiss,* No. 95B; *Reifenberg,* No. 174; *Meshorer,* No. 182; *Hill,* p. 290, No. 13.

102. Æ denarius. 133/134 C.E. 2.95 gr. 18 mm.

Obverse:

Wreath tied at bottom, with almond-shaped leaves; above, a kind of medallion closing wreath. Border of dots.

Legend within, in two lines: שמעון (Shimʿon).

Reverse:

Upright palm branch, bent to left at tip. Border of dots.

Legend, around from lower right: ש(נת) ב׳ לחר(ות) יש(ר)אל (Y[ear] 2 of the Free[dom] of Is[r]ael).

Bibliography: *Narkiss*, No. 106D; *Reifenberg*, No. 175; *Meshorer*, No. 204; *Hill*, p. 297, Nos. 61–65.

103. Æ denarius. 133/134 C.E. 3.05 gr. 18 mm.

Obverse:

Bunch of grapes hanging on branch with small leaf at left. Border of dots.

Legend, in semi-circle downward from left to right: שמעון (Shimʿon).

Traces of previous striking: ΛN.V CEB.

Reverse:

Elongated lyre (very small) with three strings. Border of dots.

Legend, around from lower right: ש(נת) ב׳ לחר(ות) ישאל (Y[ear] 2 of the Free[dom] of Is[r]ael).

Bibliography: *Narkiss*, No. 92B; *Reifenberg*, No. 178; *Meshorer*, No. 187; *Hill*, p. 291, No. 20.

104. Æ denarius. 133/134 C.E. 2.85 gr. 18 mm.

Obverse:

Bunch of grapes hanging on branch with small leaf at left. Border of dots.

Legend, in semi-circle downward from left to right: שמעון (Shimʿon).

Reverse:

Upright palm branch, bent to left at tip. Border of dots.

Legend, around from lower right: ש(נת) ב׳ לחר(ות) ישאל (!) (Y[ear] 2 of the Free[dom] of Is[r]ael).

Bibliography: *Narkiss*, No. 92A; *Reifenberg*, No. 179; *Meshorer*, No. 189; *Hill*, pp. 291–292, Nos. 21–27.

105. Æ large bronze. 133/134 C.E. 18.80 gr. 31/32 mm.

Obverse:
Wreath tied at bottom, with leaves in groups of two; above, a kind of medallion closing wreath. Border of dots.
Legend within, in two lines: שמ/עון (Shim'on).

Reverse:
Large amphora with ribbed body, two handles, and high base. Border of dots.
Legend, around from lower right: ש(נת) ב' לחר(ות) ישראל (Y[ear] 2 of the Free[dom] of Israel).

Bibliography: *Narkiss*, No. 98; *Reifenberg*, No. 197; *Meshorer*, No. 192.

106. Æ large bronze. 42.70 gr. 31/32 mm.

A city coin or Roman sestertius, prepared for restriking by the Bar Kokhba authorities. The design has been entirely obliterated on both faces by hammering. Probably intended for a large bronze of the wreath/amphora type.

107. Æ medium bronze A. 133/134 C.E. 10.70 gr. 24/26 mm.

Obverse:
Palm-tree with seven branches and two bunches of dates. Border of dots.
Legend, in field flanking in two lines: שמעו(ן) (Shim'on). Traces of previous striking IΔH (?).

Reverse:
Vine-leaf hanging from branch. Border of dots.
Legend, around from upper left: ש(נת) ב' לחר(ות) שיראל(!) (Y[ear] 2 of the Free[dom] of Israel).
Traces of previous striking: top of Hadrian's head and legend: KAITPA.

Bibliography: *Narkiss*, No. 99; *Reifenberg*, No. 200; *Meshorer*, No. 195; *Hill*, 306–309, Nos. 29–60.

ISSUE ENTITLED "ELEAZAR THE PRIEST"/"YEAR 2 OF THE FREEDOM OF ISRAEL"

108. Æ small bronze. 133/134 C.E. 2.55 gr. 18/20 mm.

Obverse:
Palm-tree with seven branches and two bunches of dates. Border of dots. Legend, in field flanking in three lines: אלעזר הכהן (Eleazar the Priest).

Reverse:
Bunch of grapes hanging from branch. Border of dots.
Legend, around from left: ש(נת) ב' לחר(ות) ישראל(!) (Year [2] of the Free[d]om of Is[r]ael).

Bibliography: *Narkiss*, No. 103; *Reifenberg*, No. 196; *Meshorer*, No. 197.

ISSUE ENTITLED "JERUSALEM"/"YEAR 2 OF THE FREEDOM OF ISRAEL

109. Æ small bronze. 133/134 C.E. 4.70 gr. 19/21 mm.

Obverse:
Palm-tree with seven branches and two bunches of dates. Border of dots. Legend, in field flanking in two lines: י רו/של ם (Jerusalem).

Reverse:
Bunch of grapes hanging from branch. Border of dots.
Legend, around from upper right: ש(נת) ב' לחר(ות) ישראל(!) (Y[ear] 2 of the Free[dom] of Is[r]ael).

Bibliography: *Narkiss*, No. 102; *Reifenberg*, No. 202; *Meshorer*, No. 198; *Hill*, p. 310, Nos. 63–65.

110. Æ denarius. 134/135 C.E. 3.90 gr. 19 mm.

Obverse:

Wreath tied at bottom, with almond-shaped leaves; above, a kind of medallion closing wreath. Border of dots.

Legend within, in two lines: שמעון (Shim'on).

Reverse:

Juglet with ribbed body, stem, and handle; in field on upper right, small palm branch. Border of dots.

Legend, around from lower right: לחרות ירושלם (For the Freedom of Jerusalem).

Bibliography: *Narkiss*, No. 106A; *Reifenberg*, No. 181; *Meshorer*, No. 202; *Hill*, pp. 292–295, Nos. 28–38, 41–45, 47.

111. Æ denarius. 134/135 C.E. 2.95 gr. 19/20 mm.

Obverse:

Wreath tied at bottom, with almond-shaped leaves; above, a kind of medallion closing wreath. Border of dots.

Legend within, in two lines: שמעון (Shim'on).

Reverse:

Elongated lyre with three strings. Border of dots.

Legend, around from lower right: לחרות ירושלם (For the Freedom of Jerusalem).

Bibliography: *Narkiss*, No. 106B; *Reifenberg*, No. 183; *Meshorer*, No. 205; *Hill*, p. 296, Nos. 55–58.

112. Æ denarius. 134/135 C.E. 2.95 gr. 18/19 mm.

Obverse:

Wreath tied at bottom, with almond-shaped leaves; above, a kind of medallion closing wreath. Border of dots.

Legend within, in two lines: שמעון (Shim'on).

Reverse:

Two trumpets with mouthpieces at bottom. Border of dots.

Legend, around from lower right: לחרות ירושלם (For the Freedom of Jerusalem). Traces of previous striking: head of Hadrian and legend: ... CTO ...

Bibliography: Narkiss, No. 106C; *Reifenberg*, No. 182; *Meshorer*, No. 203; *Hill*, p. 296, No. 59.

113. Æ denarius. 134/135 C.E. 2.90 gr. 19/20 mm.

Obverse:

Bunch of grapes hanging from branch. Border of dots.
Legend, in semi-circle downward from left to right: שמעון שׁ ע ס ה ל (Shim'on). Traces of previous striking: legend: GERDA (denarius of Trajan).

Reverse:

Upright palm branch, bent to left at tip. Border of dots. (Crude execution.)
Legend, around from lower right: לחרות ירושלם (For the Freedom of Jerusalem). Vague traces of previous striking.

Bibliography: *Narkiss,* No. 107D; *Reifenberg,* No. 187; *Meshorer,* No. 206; *Hill,* pp. 291–292, Nos. 21–27.

114. Æ medium bronze A. 134/135 C.E. 11.10 gr. 25/27 mm.

Obverse:

Palm-tree with seven branches and two bunches of dates. Border of dots.
Legend, in field flanking in two lines: שמעון שׁ ע ס א (Shim'on).

Reverse:

Vine-leaf on branch. Border of dots.
Legend, around from upper left: ש(נת) ב' לחר(ות) שיראל(!) (Y[ear] 2 of the Free[dom] of Israel).

Bibliography: *Narkiss,* No. 99; *Reifenberg,* No. 200; *Meshorer,* No. 195; *Hill,* pp. 306–309, Nos. 29–60.

115. Æ medium bronze B. 134/135 C.E. 5.80 gr. 19/22 mm.

Obverse:

Broad lyre with four strings. Border of dots.
Legend, around from lower right: ש(נת) ב' לחר(ות) ישראל (Y[ear] 2 of the Free[dom] of Israel).

Reverse:

Wreath tied at bottom, with leaves in groups of three; above, a kind of medallion closing wreath; within, upright palm branch.
Legend, around from lower right: לחרות ירושלם (For the Freedom of Jerusalem).

Bibliography: *Narkiss,* No. 104; *Reifenberg,* No. 201; *Meshorer,* No. 194; *Hill,* p. 310, Nos. 61–62.

ISSUES ENTITLED "SHIM'ON"/"FOR THE FREEDOM OF JERUSALEM"

116. Æ tetradrachm. 134/135 C.E. 12.55 gr. 24/25 mm.

Obverse:

Temple façade: architrave on four ribbed columns with capitals, standing on row of ashlars; between two inner columns, Ark (with shelf and scrolls ?). Star above. Border of dots.

Legend, flanking: שמ/עון (Shim'on).

Reverse:

Lulav, with small *etrog* in field on left. Border of dots.

Legend, around from lower right: לחרות ירושלם (For the Freedom of Jerusalem).

Bibliography: *Narkiss*, No. 105; *Reifenberg*, No. 167; *Meshorer*, No. 199; *Hill*, pp. 285–286, Nos. 8–17.

117. Æ tetradrachm. 134/135 C.E. 14.90 gr. 25/26 mm.

Obverse:

Temple façade, architrave on four ribbed columns with capitals, standing on row of ashlars; between two inner columns, Ark (with shelf and scrolls ?). Wavy line above. Border of dots.

Legend, flanking: שמ/עון (Shim'on).

Reverse:

Lulav, with small *etrog* in field on left. Border of dots.

Legend, around from lower right: לחרות ירושלם (For the Freedom of Jerusalem). Traces of previous striking.

Bibliography: *Narkiss*, No. 105; *Reifenberg*, No. 166; *Meshorer*, No. 201; *Hill*, p. 287, Nos. 18–20.

118. Æ tetradrachm. 134/135 C.E. 13.55 gr. 24/26 mm.

Obverse:

Temple façade: architrave on four ribbed columns with capitals, standing on rows of ashlars; between two inner columns, Ark (with shelf and scrolls ?). Wavy line above. Border of dots.

Legend, flanking: שמ/עון (Shim'on).

Reverse:

Lulav, with small *etrog* in field on left. Border of dots.

Legend, around from lower right: לחרות ירושלם (For the Freedom of Jerusalem).

Bibliography: *Narkiss*, No. 105; *Reifenberg*, No. 166; *Meshorer*, No. 201; *Hill*, p. 287, Nos. 18–20.

119. Æ tetradrachm. 134/135 C.E. 13.65 gr. 26 mm.

Obverse:

Temple façade: architrave on four ribbed columns with capitals, standing on row of ashlars; between two inner columns, Ark (with shelf and scrolls ?). Star above. Border of dots.

Legend, flanking: שמ/עון (Shimᶜon).

Traces of previous striking: ... OVE ... (coin of Vespasian).

Reverse:

Lulav (without *etrog* in this case). Border of dots.

Legend, around from lower right: לחרות ירושלם (For the Freedom of Jerusalem).

Bibliography: *Reifenberg*, No. 168; *Meshorer*, No. 200.

120. Æ denarius. 134/135 C.E. 3.65 gr. 18/19 mm.

Obverse:

Wreath tied at bottom, with almond-shaped leaves; above, a kind of medallion closing wreath. Border of dots.

Legend within, in two lines: שמ/עון (Shimᶜon).

Reverse:

Juglet with ribbed body, stem, and handle: in field on upper right, small palm branch. Border of dots.

Legend, around from lower right: לחרות ירושלם (For the Freedom of Jerusalem).

Bibliography: *Narkiss*, No. 106A; *Reifenberg*, No. 181; *Meshorer*, No. 202; *Hill*, pp. 292–295, Nos. 28–38, 41–45, 47.

121. Æ denarius. 134/135 C.E. 2.45 gr. 17/18 mm.

Obverse:

Wreath tied at bottom, with almond-shaped leaves; above, a kind of medallion closing wreath. Border of dots.

Legend within, in two lines: שמ/עון (Shimᶜon).

Reverse:

Two trumpets with mouthpieces at bottom. Dot in center. Border of dots.

Legend, around from bottom right: לחרות ירושלם (For the Freedom of Jerusalem).

Bibliography: *Narkiss*, No. 106C; *Reifenberg*, No. 182; *Meshorer*, No. 203; *Hill*, p. 296, Nos. 59–60.

122. Æ denarius. 134/135 C.E. 3.00 gr. 18/19 mm.

Obverse:
Wreath tied at bottom, with almond-shaped leaves; above, a kind of medallion closing wreath. Border of dots.
Legend within, in two lines: שמ/עון (Shim'on).

Reverse:
Upright palm branch bent to right at tip. Border of dots.
Legend, around from lower right: לחרות ירושלם (For the Freedom of Jerusalem).

Bibliography: *Narkiss*, No. 106D; *Reifenberg*, No. 183; *Meshorer*, No. 204; *Hill*, p. 297, Nos. 61–65.

123. Æ denarius. 134/135 C.E. 2.25 gr. 20 mm.

Obverse:
Wreath tied at bottom, with almond-shaped leaves; above, a kind of medallion closing wreath. Dot in center. Border of dots.
Legend within, in two lines: שמ/עון (Shim'on).

Traces of previous striking: GERDAC (denarius of Trajan).

Reverse:
Juglet with ribbed body, stem, and handle; in field on upper right, small palm branch. Border of dots.
Legend, around from lower right: לחרות ירושלם (For the Freedom of Jerusalem). Traces of previous striking: RINC.

Bibliography: *Narkiss*, No. 106A; *Reifenberg*, No. 181; *Meshorer*, No. 202; *Hill*, pp. 292–295, Nos. 28–38, 41–45, 47.

124. Æ denarius. 134/135 C.E. 3.30 gr. 19 mm.

Obverse:
Wreath tied at bottom, with almond-shaped leaves; above, a kind of medallion closing wreath. Dot in center. Border of dots.
Legend within, in two lines: שמ/עון (Shim'on).

Reverse:
Juglet with ribbed body, stem, and handle (without palm branch in field). Border of dots.
Legend, around from lower right: לחרות ירושלם (For the Freedom of Jerusalem).

Bibliography: *Meshorer*, No. 202A; *Hill*, p. 294, Nos. 39–40, 46.

125. Æ denarius. 134/135 C.E. 3.00 gr. 18 mm.

Obverse:

Wreath tied at bottom, with almond-shaped leaves; above, a kind of medallion closing wreath. Dot in center. Border of dots.
Legend, within, in two lines: שמעון (Shim'on).
Traces of previous striking: CEB ΓEP.

Reverse:

Elongated lyre with three strings. Border of dots.
Legend, around from right: לחרות ירושלם (For the Freedom of Jerusalem).
Traces of previous striking: ΥΠΑΤC (drachm of Trajan).

Bibliography: *Narkiss,* No. 106B; *Reifenberg,* No. 184; *Meshorer,* No. 205; *Hill,* pp. 295–298, Nos. 48–58.

126. Æ denarius. 134/135 C.E. 2.90 gr. 17 mm.

Obverse:

Wreath tied at bottom, with almond-shaped leaves; above, a kind of medallion closing wreath. Dot in center. Border of dots. (Crude execution.)
Legend within, in two lines: שמעון (Shim'on).

Reverse:

Elongated lyre with three strings. Border of dots. (Crude execution.) Dot on central string.
Legend, around from lower right: לחרות (יר)ושלם (For the Freedom of Jerusalem).

Bibliography: *Narkiss,* No. 106B; *Reifenberg,* No. 184; *Meshorer,* No. 205; *Hill,* pp. 295–296, Nos. 48–58.

127. Æ denarius. 134/135 C.E. 3.25 gr. 17/18 mm.

Obverse:

Wreath tied at bottom, with almond-shaped leaves; above, a kind of medallion closing wreath. Dot in center. Border of dots.
Legend within, in two lines: שמעון (Shim'on).
Traces of previous striking: –VS–

Reverse:

Upright palm branch, bent to right at tip. Border of dots.
Legend, around from lower right: לחרות ירושלם (For the Freedom of Jerusalem).

Bibliography: *Narkiss,* No. 106D; *Reifenberg,* No. 183; *Meshorer,* No. 204; *Hill,* p. 297, Nos. 61–65.

128. Æ denarius. 134/135 C.E. 2.80 gr. 19/20 mm.

Obverse:
Bunch of grapes hanging from branch. Border of dots.
Legend, in semi-circle downward from left to right: ᵓ⅄ο⅄ω שמעון (Shimʿon). Traces of previous striking: TSN.

Reverse:
Juglet with ribbed body, stem, and handle; in field on upper right, small palm branch. Border of dots.
Legend, around from lower right: ᵓ⅃ωᴧ⅄ᴦᴦ⅄ᴧ⅄⅂⅃ לחרות ירושלם (For the Freedom of Jerusalem).

Bibliography: *Narkiss*, No. 107A; *Reifenberg*, No. 185; *Meshorer*, No. 207; *Hill*, pp. 297–298, Nos. 66–68.

129. Æ denarius. 134/135 C.E. 3.15 gr. 18/19 mm.

Obverse:
Bunch of grapes hanging from branch. Border of dots.
Legend, in semi-circle downward from left to right: ᵓ⅄οᴄω שמעון (Shimʿon).

Reverse:
Juglet with ribbed body, stem and handle; in field on upper right, small palm branch. Border of dots.
Legend, around from lower right: ᵓ⅃ωᴧ⅄ᴦᴦ⅄ᴧ⅄⅂⅃ לחרות ירושלם (For the Freedom of Jerusalem).
Traces of previous striking: AIANO KAICAP (coin of Trajan).

Bibliography: *Narkiss*, No. 107A; *Reifenberg*, No. 185; *Meshorer*, No. 207; *Hill*, pp. 297–298, Nos. 66–68.

130. Æ denarius. 134/135 C.E. 2.85 gr. 20/21 mm.

Obverse:
Bunch of grapes hanging from branch. Border of dots.
Legend, in semi-circle downward from left to right: ᵓ⅄οᴄω שמען (Shimʿon).

Reverse:
Juglet with ribbed body, stem, and handle (without palm branch). Border of dots.
Legend, around from lower right: ᵓ⅃ωᴧ⅄ᴦᴦ⅄ᴧ⅄⅂⅃ לחרות ירושלם (For the Freedom of Jerusalem).

Bibliography: *Hill*, p. 297, No. 66.

131. Æ denarius. 134/135 C.E. 3.45 gr. 19/20 mm.

Obverse:

Bunch of grapes hanging from branch. Border of dots.
Legend, in semi-circle downward from left to right: שמעון ‎ש ‎ו ‎ע ‎ו ‎ן
(Shim'on). Traces of previous striking: ... A. NVS.

Reverse:

Elongated lyre with three strings. Border of dots.
Legend, around from lower right: לחרות ירושלם ‎ל ‎ח ‎ר ‎ו ‎ת ‎י ‎ר ‎ו ‎ש ‎ל ‎ם
(For the Freedom of Jerusalem). Vague traces of previous striking.

Bibliography: *Narkiss,* No. 107B; *Reifenberg,* No. 188; *Meshorer,* No. 209; *Hill,* pp. 298–300, Nos. 69–84.

132. Æ denarius. 134/135 C.E. 2.95 gr. 18 mm.

Obverse:

Bunch of grapes hanging from branch. Border of dots.
Legend, in semi-circle downward from left to right: שמעון ‎ש ‎ו ‎ע ‎ו ‎ן
(Shim'on).

Reverse:

Two trumpets with mouthpieces at bottom. Border of dots.
Legend, around from lower right: לחרות ירושלם ‎ל ‎ח ‎ר ‎ו ‎ת ‎י ‎ר ‎ו ‎ש ‎ל ‎ם
(For the Freedom of Jerusalem).

Bibliography: *Narkiss,* No. 107C; *Reifenberg,* No. 186; *Meshorer,* No. 208; *Hill,* pp. 300–301, Nos. 85–93.

133. Æ denarius. 134/135 C.E. 3.25 gr. 18/19 mm.

Obverse:

Bunch of grapes hanging from branch. Border of dots.
Legend, in semi-circle downward from left to right: שמעון ‎ש ‎ו ‎ע ‎ו ‎ן
(Shim'on). Traces of previous striking: ... ER (coin of Trajan).

Reverse:

Upright palm branch, slightly bent to right. Border of dots.
Legend, around from lower left: לחרות ירושלם ‎ל ‎ח ‎ר ‎ו ‎ת ‎י ‎ר ‎ו ‎ש ‎ל ‎ם
(For the Freedom of Jerusalem).
Vague traces of previous striking at lower end of palm branch.

Bibliography: *Narkiss,* No. 107D; *Reifenberg,* No. 187; *Meshorer,* No. 206; *Hill,* pp. 291–292, Nos. 21–27.

134. Æ denarius. 134/135 C.E. 3.20 gr. 18/19 mm.

Obverse:
Bunch of grapes hanging from branch. Border of dots.
Legend, around from left: ﬦﬡﬠﬥﬧ שמעון (Shim‘on).

Reverse:
Upright palm branch, slightly bent to right. Border of dots.
Legend, around from lower right: ﬥﬡﬧﬦﬥﬡﬧﬠ לחרות ירושלם
(For the Freedom of Jerusalem).

Bibliography: *Narkiss*, No. 97C; *Reifenberg*, No. 187, *Meshorer*, No. 189; *Hill*, p. 292, Nos. 24–25.

135. Æ medium bronze A. 134/135 C.E. 11.60 gr. 29/32 mm.

Obverse:
Palm-tree with seven branches and two bunches of dates. Border of dots.
Legend, in field flanking in two lines: ﬠﬡﬦ שמעון (Shim‘on).

Reverse:
Vine-leaf hanging from branch. Border of dots.
Legend, around from upper left: ﬥﬡﬧﬠﬧﬦ לחרות ירושלם
(For the Freedom of Jerusalem).

Bibliography: *Narkiss*, No. 108; *Reifenberg*, No. 204; *Meshorer*, No. 211; *Hill*, pp. 311–313, Nos. 66–92.

136. Æ medium bronze A. 134/135 C.E. 11.70 gr. 24/25 mm.

Obverse:
Palm-tree with seven branches and two bunches of dates. Border of dots.
Legend, in field flanking in two lines: ﬠﬡﬦ שמעון (Shim‘on).

Reverse:
Vine-leaf hanging from branch. Border of dots.
Legend, around from upper left: ﬥﬡﬧﬠﬧﬦ לחרות ירושלם
(For the Freedom of Jerusalem).
Traces of previous striking at edge of vine-leaf: head of emperor.

Bibliography: *Narkiss*, No. 108; *Reifenberg*, No. 204; *Meshorer*, No. 211; *Hill*, pp. 311–313, Nos. 66–92.

137. Æ medium bronze A. 134/135 C.E. 6.70 gr. 25/26 mm.

Obverse:

Palm-tree with seven branches and two bunches of dates. Border of dots.
Legend, in field flanking in two lines: ⅄ o ⅁ ш שמעון (Shimʿon).

Traces of previous striking in field left below: NT (?).

Reverse:

Vine-leaf hanging from branch. Border of dots.
Legend, around from upper left: ⅄/ш⅄ף⅂ꓕ×⅄ף ⊟⅂ לחרות ירושלם (For the Freedom of Jerusalem).

Bibliography: *Narkiss*, No. 108; *Reifenberg*, No. 204; *Meshorer*, No. 211; *Hill*, pp. 311–313, Nos. 66–92.

138. Æ medium bronze B. 134/135 C.E. 6.75 gr. 20/22 mm.

Obverse:

Elongated lyre with three strings. Border of dots.
Legend, flanking: ⅁ ш
ꓹ⅄o שמעון (Shimʿon).

(At right of lyre, incuse letter ⊟ (ח) from the legend לחרות ירושלים caused by mis-strike of reverse.)

Reverse:

Wreath tied at bottom, with leaves in groups of three; above, a kind of medallion closing wreath; within, upright palm branch.
Legend, around from lower right: ⅄/ш⅄ף⅂ꓕ×⅄ף⊟⅂ לחרות ירושלם (For the Freedom of Jerusalem).

Bibliography: *Narkiss*, No. 109; *Reifenberg*, No. 205; *Meshorer*, No. 212; *Hill*, p. 314, Nos. 93–98.

139. Æ small bronze. 134/135 C.E. 4.75 gr. 19/20 mm.

Obverse:

Palm-tree with seven branches and two bunches of dates. Border of dots.
Legend, in field flanking: o ⅁ ш ⅄ ꓹ שמעון (Shimʿon).

Reverse:

Bunch of grapes hanging from branch. Border of dots.
Legend, from upper left: ⅂ш⅄ף⅂ ꓕ×⅄ף⊟⅂ לחרות ירושל(ם) (For the Freedom of Jerusale[m]).

Bibliography: *Narkiss*, No. 110; *Reifenberg*, No. 206; *Meshorer*, No. 215; *Hill*, pp. 314–315, Nos. 99–108.

ISSUE ENTITLED "ELEAZAR THE PRIEST"/"FOR THE FREEDOM OF JERUSALEM"

140. Æ small bronze. 134/135 C.E. 5.35 gr. 18/19 mm.

Obverse:
Palm-tree with seven branches and two bunches of dates. Border of dots.
Legend, in field flanking in three lines:

אלעזר הכהן (Eleazar the Priest).

Reverse:
Bunch of grapes hanging from branch. Border of dots.
Legend, around from upper left: לחרות ירושל(ם)
(For the Freedom of Jerusale[m]).

Bibliography: *Narkiss*, No. 111; *Reifenberg*, No. 203; *Meshorer*, No. 213.

ISSUES ENTITLED "JERUSALEM"/"FOR THE FREEDOM OF JERUSALEM"

141. Æ small bronze. 134/135 C.E. 6.35 gr. 19 mm.

Obverse:
Palm-tree with seven branches and two bunches of dates. Border of dots.
Legend, in field flanking in two lines: ירו/שלם (Jerusalem).

Reverse:
Bunch of grapes hanging from branch. Border of dots.
Legend, around from upper left: לחרות ירושל(ם)
(For the Freedom of Jerusale[m]).

Bibliography: *Narkiss*, No. 112; *Reifenberg*, No. 207; *Meshorer*, No. 214; *Hill*, p. 316, Nos. 109–111.

92

142. Æ small bronze. 134/135 C.E. 3.70 gr. 17 mm.

Obverse:

Palm-tree with seven branches and two bunches of dates. Border of dots. Legend, in field flanking in two lines: ירו/שלם (Jerusalem).

Reverse:

Bunch of grapes hanging from branch. Border of dots. Legend, around from upper right: לחרות ירושל(ם) (For the Freedom of Jerusale[m]).

Bibliography: *Narkiss*, No. 112; *Reifenberg*, No. 207; *Meshorer*, No. 214; *Hill*, p. 316, Nos. 109–111.

no. 141

VII. THE ROMAN PROCURATORS
(6–41, 44–66 C.E.)

With the banishment of Herod Archelaus in 6 C.E., Roman penetration into Eretz Israel became complete. The territory ruled by Archelaus – Samaria, Judea, and Idumea – now came under direct Roman administration, based at Caesarea. This administration was headed by a procurator, who was responsible to the Roman governor of the province of Syria, and Eretz Israel was thus annexed to the Provincia Syria. During the period in question (the continuity of which was broken only by the reign of Agrippa I), there were 14 procurators, most of whom held office for short terms, though several (especially in the reign of Tiberius) were here for fairly long periods. Thus, Valerius Gratus served for 12 years and Pontius Pilate for 11 years.

The administration of Eretz Israel by the procurators – men often ignorant of its specific problems, which stemmed from the social and cultural differences between Rome and Jerusalem – eventually led to major disturbances in the era of the last procurator, Gessius Florus (66 C.E.), and these developed into the First Jewish Revolt against Rome (66–70 C.E.).

The coins struck under the procurators all had the same denomination – the perutah, a small bronze coin in widest use in the country. These coins do not bear the imperial portrait, only the emperor's name. The designs are generally floral: palm-tree, palm branch, crossed palm branches, ear of corn, three ears of corn, wreath, olive sprig, three lilies, or vine-leaf. Other designs include the double cornucopia, goblet, amphora, and crossed shield and spears. Only Pontius Pilate issued coins bearing pagan cultic utensils, such as the lituus (augur's wand) and simpulum (libation ladle).

The procuratorial coins are all dated according to the regnal years of the emperors under whom they were issued, and their dates of issue are readily ascertained. The procuratorial coins are given here in chronological sequence; the following procurators did not issue coins: under Augustus – Annius Rufus (12–15 C.E.); under Tiberius – Marcellus (36–37 C.E.); under Gaius Caligula – Marullus (37–41 C.E.); under Claudius – Cuspius Fadus (44 C.E. ?); Tiberius Alexander (48 C.E. ?); Ventidius Cumanus (48–52 C.E.); and of the later procurators: Porcius Festus (60–62 C.E.); Albinus (62–64 C.E.), and Gessius Florus (64–66 C.E.).

UNDER AUGUSTUS

COPONIUS (6–9 C.E.)

143. Æ perutah. 5/6 C.E. 2.75 gr. 17/18 mm.

Obverse:
Ear of barley. Border of dots.
Legend, around from lower left: KAICAPOC (Caesar). Struck off-center.

Reverse:
Palm-tree with eight branches and two bunches of dates. Border of dots.
Legend, across field, date: L Λς (36th year [of Augustus' reign, 5/6 C.E.]).

Bibliography: *Narkiss* II, No. 199; *Reifenberg*, No. 118; *Meshorer*, No. 216; *Hill*, p. 248, Nos. 1–8.

no. 143

MARCUS AMBIBULUS (9–12 C.E.)

144. Æ perutah. 8/9 C.E. 2.05 gr. 16 mm.

Obverse:
Ear of barley. Border of dots.
Legend, around from lower left: KAICAPOC (Caesar).

Reverse:
Palm-tree with eight branches and two bunches of dates. Border of dots.
Legend, across field, date: L ΛΘ (39th year [of Augustus' reign, 8/9 C.E.])

Bibliography: *Narkiss* II, No. 199; *Reifenberg*, No. 119; *Meshorer*, No. 217; *Hill*, pp. 248–249, Nos. 9–16.

145. Æ perutah. 10/11 C.E. 2.40 gr. 16/17 mm.

Obverse:
Ear of barley. Border of dots.
Legend, around from lower left: KAICAPOC (Caesar).

Reverse:
Palm-tree with eight branches and two bunches of dates. Border of dots.
Legend, across field, date: L MA (41st year [of Augustus' reign, 10/11 C.E.]).

Bibliography: *Narkiss* II, No. 199; *Reifenberg*, No. 121; *Meshorer*, No. 219; *Hill*, pp. 249–250, Nos. 20–27.

UNDER TIBERIUS

VALERIUS GRATUS (15–26 C.E.)

146. Æ **perutah. 15/16 C.E. 2.00 gr. 15/16 mm.**

Obverse:
Wreath, tied at bottom. Border of dots.
Legend within, in two lines: KAI/CAP (Caesar).

Reverse:
Double cornucopia. Border of dots.
Legend within: TIB/LB (Tiberius, 2nd year [of his reign, 15/16 C.E.]).

Bibliography: *Narkiss* II, No. 200; *Reifenberg*, No. 122; *Meshorer*, No. 220; *Hill*, p. 251, Nos. 1–3.

147. Æ **perutah. 15/16 C.E. 1.60 gr. 16 mm.**

Obverse:
Wreath tied on lower right.
Legend within, in two lines: IOY/ΛIA (Julia [Livia, Tiberius' mother]).

Reverse:
Olive branch. Border of dots.
Legend, across field, date: L B (2nd year [of Tiberius' reign, 15/16 C.E.]).

Bibliography: *Narkiss* II, No. 201; *Reifenberg*, No. 123; *Meshorer*, No. 221; *Hill*, pp. 251–252, Nos. 4–9.

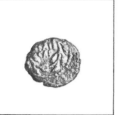

148. Æ perutah. 16/17 C.E. 1.45 gr. 14/15 mm.

Obverse:

Double cornucopia; between them, caduceus. Border of dots.
Legend, around from upper left: TIBE[P]IO[Y] (Of Tiberius); in field flanking, date: L Γ (3rd year [of Tiberius' reign, 16/17 C.E.]).

Reverse:

Wreath tied above; below, a kind of medallion closing wreath. Border of dots.
Legend within, in two lines: KAI/CAP (Caesar).
Struck off-center.

Bibliography: *Narkiss* II, No. 202; *Reifenberg*, No. 124; *Meshorer*, No. 222; *Hill*, p. 252, Nos. 10–15.

149. Æ perutah. 16/17 C.E. 1.95 gr. 15/18 mm.

Obverse:

Wreath tied above; below, a kind of medallion closing wreath. Border of dots.
Legend within, in two lines: IOV/ΛIA (Julia [Livia, Tiberius' mother]).
Struck off-center.

Reverse:

Three lilies stemming from between two leaves. Border of dots.
Legend, in field flanking, date: L Γ (3rd year [of Tiberius' reign, 16/17 C.E.]).

Bibliography: *Narkiss* II, No. 203; *Reifenberg*, No. 125; *Meshorer*, No. 223; *Hill*, p. 253, Nos. 16–22.

150. Æ perutah. 17/18 C.E. 1.30 gr. 15/16 mm.

Obverse:

Vine-leaf hanging from branch with small bunch of grapes and tendril. Border of dots.

Legend, from left to right above vine-leaf: TIBEPIOY (Of Tiberius).

Reverse:

Kantharos (tankard) with cover, foot, and two large handles. Border of dots.

Legend, from left to right above cover of kantharos: KAICAP (Caesar): in field, flanking, date: L Δ (4th year [of Tiberius' reign, 17/18 C.E.]).

Bibliography: *Narkiss* II, No. 204; *Reifenberg*, No. 126; *Meshorer*, No. 225; *Hill*, pp. 253–254, Nos. 23–26.

151. Æ perutah. 17/18 C.E. 1.75 gr. 14/15 mm.

Obverse:

Vine-branch from which stem two leaves and tendril. Border of dots.

Legend, above from left to right above vine-branch: IOYΛIA (Julia [Livia, Tiberius' mother]).

Reverse:

Narrow amphora on high base, with two handles and cover having tall handle. Border of dots.

Legend, flanking, date: L Δ (4th year [of Tiberius' reign, 17/18 C.E.]).

Bibliography: *Narkiss* II, No. 205; *Reifenberg*, No. 127; *Meshorer*, No. 224; *Hill*, p. 254, Nos. 27–30.

152. Æ perutah. 17/18 C.E. 1.90 gr. 15/16 mm.

Obverse:

Wreath tied at bottom, with leaves in groups of two. Border of dots.

Legend, within in three lines: TI[B]/KA[I]/CAP (Tiberius Caesar).

Reverse:

Upright palm-branch slightly bent to right at tip. Border of dots.

Legend, in field flanking in two lines: [I]OY ΛIA/L Δ (Julia [Livia, Tiberius' mother]; 4th year [of Tiberius' reign, 17/18 C.E.)].

Bibliography: *Narkiss* II, No. 206; *Reifenberg*, No. 128; *Meshorer*, No. 226; *Hill*, pp. 254–255, Nos. 31–36.

153. Æ perutah. 17/18 C.E. 2.30 gr. 15/16 mm.

Obverse:

Wreath tied at bottom, with leaves in groups of two. Border of dots. Legend, within wreath in three lines: TIB/KAI/CAP (Tiberius Caesar). Struck off-center.

Reverse:

Upright palm branch, slightly bent to right at tip. Border of dots. Legend, in field flanking in two lines: [I]OY ΛIA/L Δ (Julia [Livia, Tiberius' mother]; 4th year [of Tiberius' reign, 17/18 C.E.]).

Bibliography: *Narkiss* II, No. 206; *Reifenberg*, No. 128; *Meshorer*, No. 226; *Hill*, pp. 254–255, Nos. 31–36.

154. Æ perutah. 18/19 C.E. 2.25 gr. 15/16 mm.

Obverse:

Wreath tied at bottom, with leaves in groups of two. Border of dots. Legend within, in three lines: TIB/KAI/CAP (Tiberius Caesar). Struck off-center.

Reverse:

Upright palm branch, slightly bent to right at tip. Border of dots. Legend, in field flanking in two lines: IOY ΛIA/L E. (Julia [Livia, Tiberius' mother]; 5th year [of Tiberius' reign, 18/19 C.E.]).

Bibliography: *Narkiss* II, No. 206; *Reifenberg*, No. 129; *Meshorer*, No. 227; *Hill*, pp. 255–256, Nos. 38–45.

155. Æ perutah. 24/25 C.E. 2.00 gr. 15/16 mm.

Obverse:

Wreath tied at bottom, with leaves in groups of two. Border of dots.
Legend within, in three lines: TIB/KAI/CAP (Tiberius Caesar).
Struck off-center.

Reverse:

Upright palm branch, slightly bent to right at tip. Border of dots.
Legend, in field flanking in two lines: [IOY] ΛIA/L IA (Julia [Livia,
Tiberius' mother]; 11th year [of Tiberius' reign, 24/25 C.E.]).

Bibliography: *Narkiss* II, No. 206; *Reifenberg*, No. 130; *Meshorer*, No. 228; *Hill*, pp. 256–257, Nos. 46–53.

no. 149

101

PONTIUS PILATE (26–36 C.E.)

156. Æ perutah. 29/30 C.E. 1.90 gr. 15/16 mm.

Obverse:
Simpulum (libation ladle). Border of dots.
Legend, around from lower left: TIBEPIOY KAICAPOC L IS
(Of Tiberius Caesar, 16th year [of his reign, 29/30 C.E.]).

Reverse:
Three ears of barley, tied together, outer ones drooping. Border of dots.
Legend, around from upper left: IOYΛIA KAICAPOC (Empress Julia [Livia, Tiberius' mother]).

Bibliography: *Narkiss* II, No. 207; *Reifenberg*, No. 131; *Meshorer*, No. 229; *Hill*, pp. 257–258, Nos. 54–68.

no. 156

157. Æ perutah. 29/30 C.E. 2.75 gr. 14/16 mm.

Obverse:

Lituus (augur's wand). Border of dots.
Legend, around from lower left: TIBEPIOY KAICAPOC.

Reverse:

Wreath tied at bottom, with leaves in groups of two. Border of dots.
Legend within: L IS (16th year [of Tiberius' reign, 29/30 C.E.]).

Bibliography: *Narkiss* II, No. 208; *Meshorer*, No. 230A; *Hill*, p. 259, Nos. 74–77.

158. Æ perutah. 30/31 C.E. 1.90 gr. 14 mm.

Obverse:

Lituus (augur's wand). Border of dots.
Legend, around from lower left: TIBEPIOY KAICAPOC.

Reverse:

Wreath tied at bottom, with leaves in groups of two. Border of dots.
Legend within: L IZ (17th year [of Tiberius' reign, 30/31 C.E.]).

Bibliography: *Narkiss* II, No. 208; *Reifenberg*, No. 132; *Meshorer*, No. 230; *Hill*, pp. 258–259, Nos. 69–73.

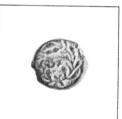

159. Æ perutah. 31/32 C.E. 2.25 gr. 15 mm.

Obverse:

Lituus (augur's wand). Border of dots.
Legend, around from lower left: TIBEPIOY KAICA[POC].

Reverse:

Wreath tied at bottom, with leaves in groups of two. Border of dots.
Legend within: L IH (18th year [of Tiberius' reign, 31/32 C.E.]).

Bibliography: *Narkiss* II, No. 208; *Reifenberg*, No. 133; *Meshorer*, No. 231; *Hill*, pp. 259–260, Nos. 78–82.

UNDER CLAUDIUS

ANTONIUS FELIX (52–60 C.E.)

160. Æ **perutah. 54 C.E. 2.85 gr. 16 mm.**

Obverse:
Two crossed palm branches. Border of dots.
Legend, around from upper right: [TI ΚΛΑΥΔΙΟϹ] ΚΑΙϹΑΡ ΓΕΡΜ (Tiberius Claudius Caesar Germanicus); below, between branches: L ΙΔ (14th year [of his reign, 54 C.E.]).

Reverse:
Wreath tied at bottom, with leaves in groups of two. Border of dots.
Legend within, in four lines: ΙΟΥ/ΛΙΑΑΓ/ΡΙΠΠΙ/ΝΑ (Julia Agrippina [Claudius' wife]). Struck off-center.

Bibliography: *Narkiss* II, No. 209; *Reifenberg*, No. 134; *Meshorer*, No. 232; *Hill*, pp. 261–263, Nos. 1–20.

no. 160

161. Æ perutah. 54 C.E. 3.00 gr. 16/17 mm.

Obverse:

Two elongated shields and two spears, crossed. Border of dots.
Legend, around from lower left: [NEPΩ KΛ]AY KAIC[AP]
(Nero Claudius Caesar [Claudius' son]).

Reverse:

Palm-tree with seven branches and two bunches of dates. Border of dots.
Struck off-center.
Legend, above: [BPIT] (Britannicus [Claudius' second son]): in field flanking
in two lines: L IΔ/K AI (14th year [of Claudius' reign, 54 C.E.]).

Bibliography: *Narkiss* II, No. 210; *Reifenberg*, No. 135; *Meshorer*, No. 233; *Hill*, pp. 264–265, Nos. 21–33.

162. Æ perutah. 54 C.E. 2.50 gr. 16/17 mm.

Obverse:

Two elongated shields and two spears, crossed. Border of dots.
Legend, around from lower left: NEPW KΛAY KAI[CAP]. (Nero Claudius
[Claudius' son]

Reverse:

Palm-tree with seven branches and two bunches of dates. Border of dots.
Legend, above: BP[IT] (Britannicus [Claudius' second son]; in field flanking
in two lines: L IΔ/K AI (14th year [of Claudius' reign, 54 C.E.]; Caesar).

Bibliography: *Narkiss* II, No. 210; *Reifenberg*, No. 135; *Meshorer*, No. 233; *Hill*, pp. 264–265, Nos. 21–33.

UNDER NERO

ANTONIUS FELIX (52–60 C.E.)

163. Æ perutah. 58/59 C.E. 2.65 gr. 15/17 mm.

Obverse:
Wreath tied at bottom, with leaves in groups of two; above, a kind of medallion closing wreath.
Legend within, in three lines: NEP/WNO/C (Nero).

Reverse:
Upright palm branch. Border of dots.
Legend, around from lower left: [L]E KAI[C]APOC (5th year [of Nero's reign, 58/59 C.E.]; Caesar).

Bibliography: *Narkiss* II, No. 211; *Reifenberg*, No. 136; *Meshorer*, No. 234; *Hill*, pp. 266–268, Nos. 1–28.

no. 163

VIII. THE ROMAN ADMINISTRATION IN ERETZ ISRAEL AFTER THE DESTRUCTION OF THE SECOND TEMPLE (70 C.E.)

The destruction of the Second Temple symbolizes the end of Jewish independence in ancient Eretz Israel; and the Flavian emperors were especially proud of their victory over the Jews.

The Romans fully exploited the propaganda value of their coins, the supreme example being the "Judaea Capta" series, issued in large quantities from the central mint at Rome (and probably at Caesarea). Vespasian may have ordered the city mints in Eretz Israel to restrict their operations, so as to encourage the use of Roman administrative issues. The coins struck here in his name, and later in the name of his son, Titus, bear Greek legends – translations of the Latin "Judaea Capta" inscriptions. They bear symbols of the Roman victory, such as a trophy with a captive Jew, symbolizing the vanquished Jewish nation, or Nike (the goddess of victory) near a palm-tree, symbolic of Judea.

Titus placed the Tenth Roman Legion in Eretz Israel as an army of occupation, stationing it within the walls of Jerusalem. Occasionally today we find coins bearing countermarks of this legion – the abbreviation LXF, the wild boar, or the war galley.

During the reign of Domitian, Roman administrative coin issues became common in Eretz Israel. Four series were issued at this time; the latter three are represented in the Bank of Israel Collection. These coins differ from those issued by Vespasian and Titus; their inscriptions are in Latin and no longer refer to the Roman victory. Both the legends and the designs on them glorify the victories of Domitian in Germany and Britain. Two of them (Nos 169 and 170/171) are imitations of imperial issues; only one (No. 173) is directly linked with this country, bearing the palm-tree motif.

164. Æ medium bronze. 13.10 gr. 23 mm.

Obverse:

Laureate bust of Titus to right. Border of dots.
Legend, around from upper right: ΑΥΤΟΚΡ ΤΙΤ[ΟΣ ΚΑΙΣ]ΑΡ (Imperator Titus Caesar).

Reverse:

Trophy comprising helmet and cuirass; on left, round shield and two spears; on right, two oval shields. At foot of trophy, on left: captive Jewess, weeping and kneeling to left, with hands bound behind; on right, ear-shaped shield. Border of dots.
Legend, around from lower left: ΙΟΥΔΑΙΑΣ ΕΑΛWΚΥΙΑΣ (Judea captive).

Bibliography: *Narkiss* II, No. 214; *Reifenberg*, No. 153; *Meshorer*, No. 238; *Hill*, pp. 276–277, Nos. 2–12.

165. Æ small bronze. 7.55 gr. 21 mm.

Obverse:

Laureate bust of Titus to right. Border of dots.
Legend, around from upper right: ΑΥΤΟΚΡ ΤΙΤ[ΟΣ Κ]ΑΙΣΑΡ.

Reverse:

Nike standing to right, half-draped; left foot treading upon helmet; left knee supporting oval shield on which she is writing with her right hand. On right, palm-tree. Border of dots.
Legend, around from lower left: [ΙΟΥΔΑ]ΙΑΣ ΕΑΛΩΚΥΙΑΣ.

Bibliography: *Narkiss* II, No. 215B; *Reifenberg*, No. 154; *Meshorer*, No. 237; *Hill*, pp. 277–278, Nos. 13–18.

166. Æ small bronze. 6.50 gr. 19/20 mm.

Obverse:

Laureate bust of Titus to right. Border of dots.
Legend, around from upper right: ΑΥΤΟΚ[Ρ ΤΙΤΟ]Σ ΚΑΙΣ[ΑΡ].

Reverse:

Nike standing to right, half-draped; left foot treading upon helmet; she is writing on a round shield hung from a palm-tree. Border of dots.
Legend, around from lower left: [ΙΟΥΔΑ]ΙΑΣ ΕΑΛWΚΥΙΑC.

Bibliography: *Narkiss* II, No. 215A; *Reifenberg*, No. 155; *Meshorer*, No. 236; *Hill*, pp. 278–279, Nos. 19–30.

UNDER DOMITIAN (81–96 C.E.)

167. Æ medium bronze. 13.05 gr. 22/23 mm.

Obverse:
Laureate bust of Domitian to right. Border of dots.
Legend, around from lower left: DOMITIANVS CAESAR DIVI/F[ilius] (Caesar Domitian, son of the divine).

Reverse:
Victory standing to left, right hand holding out wreath; left hand holding palm branch, leaning on left shoulder. Border of dots.
Legend, around from upper right: VICTORIA AVG[usti] (Caesar's Victory).

Bibliography: *Narkiss* II, No. 220; *Reifenberg*, No. 158; *Meshorer*, No. 245.

168. Æ small bronze. 4.20 gr. 19 mm.

Obverse:
Laureate bust of Domitian to right. Border of dots.
Legend, around from lower left: IMP(erator) DOMIT(ianus) AVG(ustus) GERM(anicus).

Reverse:
Trophy, comprising helmet and cuirass, with two oval shields and two crossed spears on each side; below, crossed greaves. Border of dots.
Legend, around from lower left: VICTOR(ia) AVG(usti).

Bibliography: *Narkiss* II, No. 221; *Reifenberg*, No. 162; *Meshorer*, No. 244; *Hill*, p. 283, Nos. 53–56.

169. Æ large bronze. 12.60 gr. 24/26 mm.

Obverse:
Laureate bust of Domitian to right. Border of dots.
Legend, around from lower left: DOMITIANVS CAES(ar) AVG(ustus) GERMANICVS.

Reverse:
Minerva, in fighting attitude, draped and wearing helmet, standing to right on galley; in left hand, round shield; right hand raised, holding spear obliquely. On right palm branch. On left, trophy, comprising helmet and cuirass, flanked by oval shields and crossed spears and oblique greaves below. On right of galley, small owl. Border of dots.

Bibliography: *Narkiss* II, No. 218; *Reifenberg*, No. 160; *Meshorer*, No. 242; *Hill*, pp. 281–282, Nos. 43–44.

170. Æ medium bronze. 11.95 gr. 23 mm.

Obverse:

Laureate bust of Domitian to left. Border of dots.

Legend, around from lower left: [DOMITIA]NVS CAES(ar) AVG(ustus) GERMANICVS.

Reverse:

Minerva standing to left, draped and wearing helmet; left hand holding round shield and spear; right hand resting upon trophy, comprising helmet and cuirass, flanked by oval shields and two crossed spears and crossed greaves below. Border of dots.

Bibliography: *Narkiss* II, No. 219; *Reifenberg*, No. 161; *Meshorer*, No. 243; *Hill*, p. 282, Nos. 45–52.

171. Æ medium bronze. 10.60 gr. 21 mm.

Obverse:

Laureate bust of Domitian to left. Border of dots.

Legend, around from lower left: DOMITIANVS CAES(ar) AVG(ustus) GERMANICVS.

Reverse:

Minerva standing to left, draped and wearing helmet; left hand holding round shield and spear; right hand resting upon trophy, comprising helmet and cuirass, flanked by oval shields and two crossed spears and crossed greaves below. Border of dots.

Bibliography: *Narkiss* II, No. 219; *Reifenberg*, No. 161; *Meshorer*, No. 243; *Hill*, p. 282, Nos. 45–52.

172. Æ small bronze. 5.50 gr. 16/17 mm.

Obverse:

Laureate bust of Domitian to right. Border of dots.

Legend, around from lower left: [IMP(erator) DOMITIANVS] AVG(ustus) GERM(anicus).

Reverse:

Victory standing to front, head turned to left, wings outspread, draped; right hand holding wreath; left hand holding small trophy resting on shoulder. Border of dots.

Bibliography: *Narkiss* II, No. 222; *Reifenberg*, No. 159; *Meshorer*, No. 241; *Hill*, p. 281, No. 42.

173. Æ large bronze. 92 C.E. 13.05 gr. 27/28 mm.

Obverse:

Crowned bust of Domitian to right. Border of dots.

Legend, around from lower left: IMP(erator) CAES(ar) DOMIT(ianus) AVG(ustus) GERM(anicus) P(ontifex) M(aximus) TR(ibunica) P(otestas) XI (Imperator Ceasar Domitian Augustus Germanicus, High Pontiff, Tribune for the eleventh time).

Reverse:

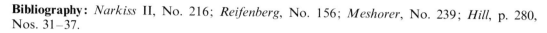

Palm-tree with seven branches and two bunches of dates. Border of dots.

Legend, around on lower right: IMP(erator) XXI CO(n)S(ul) XVI CENS(or) P(erpetuus) P(atriae) P(ater) (Imperator for the twenty-first time, Consul for the sixteenth time, perpetual Censor and Father of his Country).

Bibliography: *Narkiss* II, No. 216; *Reifenberg*, No. 156; *Meshorer*, No. 239; *Hill*, p. 280, Nos. 31–37.

174. Æ medium bronze. 93 C.E. 9.50 gr. 22/23 mm.

Obverse:

Laureate bust of Domitian to right. Border of dots.

Legend, around from lower left: IMP(erator) CAES(ar) DOMIT(ianus) AVG(ustus) GERM(anicus) P(ontifex) M(aximus) TR(ibunical) P(otestas) XII (Imperator Caesar Domitian Augustus Germanicus, High Pontiff, Tribune for the twelfth time).

Reverse:

Victory striding to left, draped, right hand holding wreath; left hand holding small trophy resting on left shoulder. Border of dots.

Legend, around from lower left: IMP(erator) XXIII CO(n)S(ul) XVI CENS(or) P(erpetuus) P(atriae) P(ater) (Imperator for the twenty-third time, Consul for the sixteenth time, perpetual Censor and Father of his Country).

Bibliography: *Narkiss* II, No. 217; *Reifenberg*, No. 157; *Meshorer*, No. 240; *Hill*, p. 281, Nos. 38–41.

175. Æ medium bronze. 93 C.E. 10.50 gr. 22/23 mm.

Obverse:
Laureate bust of Domitian to right. Border of dots.
Legend, from lower left: IMP(erator) CAES(ar) DOMIT(ianus) AVG(ustus) GERM(anicus) P(ontifex) M(aximus) TR(ibunicia) P(otestas) XII.

Reverse:
Victory striding to left, draped; right hand holding wreath; left hand holding small trophy resting on left shoulder. Border of dots.
Legend, around from lower left: IMP(erator) XXIII CO(n)S(ul) XVI CENS(or) P(erpetuus) P(atriae) P(ater).

Bibliography: *Narkiss* II, No. 217; *Reifenberg*, No. 157; *Meshorer*, No. 240; *Hill*, p. 281, Nos. 38–41.

COIN WITH COUNTERMARKS OF THE TENTH LEGION

176. Æ medium bronze. 84/85 C.E. 13.15 gr. 22/23 mm.

Obverse:
Completely worn [laureate bust of Domitian to right; border of dots.
Legend, around from upper right: IMP DOMITIAN CAESAR].
Two countermarks: (A) Bust to right within incuse circle.
　　　　　　　　　(B) LXF (Legio X Fretensis) in incuse rectangle.

Reverse:
Completely worn [Tyche, draped and wearing turreted crown, standing to left, with right foot on rock [?]; left hand leaning on long spear, right hand holding conical stone.]
Legend, around from lower left: CEBACTHNWN; in field on upper left: LΘP (109th year [of era of Sebaste, 84/85 C.E.]).
Countermark: Galley to right, with three oars and rudder – one of the Tenth Legion's emblems – within incuse rectangle.

Bibliography: De Saulcy, *Numismatique de la Terre Sainte*, Paris, 1873, p. 84, No. 2, Pl. V, No. 3; D. Barag, in "The Countermarks of the Legio Decima Fretensis," *Proceedings of the International Numismatic Convention* (Jerusalem, 1963), Tel Aviv, 1967, pp. 117–125; *Hill*, p. 78, Nos. 1–4.

IX. THE IMPERIAL "JUDAEA CAPTA" ISSUES

As previously noted, the Romans fully appreciated the value of coins as a means of propaganda. The victory over the Jews in 70 C.E. was the only great military achievement of the Emperors Vespasian and Titus, and they availed themselves of every opportunity to broadcast it. The imperial mint in Rome issued the emperor's coins, and he alone retained the right to mint gold and silver. This mint also struck coins in bronze for and with the assent of the Roman Senate, as may be ascertained from the abbreviation SC (Senatus Consulto) that appears always on Roman bronzes. A number of mints outside Rome also struck *Judaea Capta* coins, and the Bank of Israel Collection includes examples from Tarraco (Tarragona in Spain) and Lugdunum (Lyons in Gaul). The dates on these coins are based on the consular years of the emperor.

The reverse depicts a trophy, with a Jew or Jewess seated below and weeping – a symbol of the vanquished Jewish people – and a palm-tree symbolizing Judea, with the goddess of Victory.

no. 177

IMPERIAL ROMAN COINS COMMEMORATING THE VICTORY OVER JUDEA AND BEARING THE NAMES OF VESPASIAN AND TITUS (UNTIL THE DEATH OF VESPASIAN)

177. *A'* **aureus. 70 C.E. (?). 7.40 gr. 18/20 mm.**

Obverse:
Laureate head of Vespasian to right. Border of dots.
Legend, around from lower left:
IMP(erator) CAESAR VESPASIANVS AVG(ustus).

Reverse:
Captive Jewess seated on ground weeping, draped and veiled, head resting upon left hand, leaning upon knees. Behind, trophy, comprising helmet and cuirass, one oblong and one round shield, two greaves, and two shields on ground. Border of dots.
Legend, below: IVDAEA. Struck off-center.

Bibliography: *Mattingly* II, p. 6, No. 37.

178. *AR* **denarius. 70 C.E. (?). Mint of Rome. 3.20 gr. 18/19 mm.**

Obverse:
Laureate head of Vespasian to right. Border of dots.
Legend, around from lower left:
IMP(erator) CAESAR VESPASIANVS AVG(ustus).

Reverse:
Captive Jewess seated on ground weeping, draped and veiled, head resting upon left hand, leaning upon knees. Behind, trophy, comprising helmet and cuirass, one oblong and one round shield, two greaves, and two shields on ground. Border of dots.
Legend, below: IVDAEA.

Bibliography: *Mattingly* II, p. 6, No. 37.

no. 178

179. Æ denarius. 71 C.E. (?). Mint of Lugdunum. 2.95 gr. 17/18 mm.

Obverse:
Laureate head of Vespasian to right. Border of dots.
Legend, around from lower left:
IMP(erator) CAESAR VESPASIANVS AVG(ustus) TR(ibunicia) P(ostestas).

Reverse:
Captive Jewess, draped, standing to left with hands bound in front and head bowed. Behind, on right, palm-tree with six branches and two bunches of dates. Border of dots.
Legend, around from lower left: IVDAEA DEVICTA (Judea vanquished).

Bibliography: *Mattingly* II, p. 79, No. 388.

180. Æ sestertius. 71 C.E. Mint of Rome. 27.75 gr. 35 mm.

Obverse:
Laureate head of Vespasian to right. Border of dots.
Legend, around from lower left: IMP(erator) CAESAR VESPASIAN(us) AVG(ustus) P(ontifex) M(aximus) TR(ibunicia) P(otestas) P(atriae) P(ater) CO(n)S(ul) III.

Reverse:
Captive Jewess, weeping, seated on armor at right, draped and veiled, leaning head on left hand, right hand on knee. In center, tall palm-tree with five branches and two bunches of dates. On left, Titus (?) in armor standing to right, with left foot on helmet, leaning left hand on long spear (or scepter?) and holding short sword in right hand. Border of dots.
Legend, around from lower left: IVDAEA CAPTA; in exergue: S(enatus) C(onsulto).

Bibliography: *Mattingly* II, p. 117, No. 546.

181. Æ sestertius. 71 C.E. Mint of Rome. 25.30 gr. 32/34 mm.

Obverse:
Laureate head of Vespasian to right. Border of dots.
Legend, around from lower left: IMP(erator) CAES(ar) VESPAS(ianus) AVG(ustus) P(ontifex) M(aximus) TR(ibunicia) P(otestas) P(atriae) P(ater) CO(n)S(ul) III.

Reverse:
Captive Jewess, weeping, seated on armor at right, draped and veiled, leaning head on left hand, right hand on knees. In center, tall palm-tree with four branches and two bunches of dates. On left, captive Jew standing to right, with hands bound behind, and two oval shields at feet on left. Border of dots.
Legend, around from lower left: IVDAEA CAPTA; in exergue: S C.

Bibliography: *Mattingly* II, p. 115, No. 535.

182. Æ sestertius. 71 C.E. Mint of Rome. 25.90 gr. 31 mm.

Obverse:
Laureate head of Vespasian to right. Border of dots.
Legend, around from lower left: IMP(erator) CAES(ar) VESPAS(ianus) AVG(ustus) P(ontifex) M(aximus) TR(ibunicia) P(otestas) P(atriae) P(ater) CO(n)S(ul) III.

Reverse:
Victory, half-draped, standing to right, with left foot on helmet, writing on oval shield hanging on palm-tree with five branches and supported by her left knee. On right, seated captive Jewess weeping and leaning head on left hand, with right hand on knees.
Legend, around from lower left: VICTORIA AVGVSTI; in exergue: S C.

Bibliography: *Mattingly* II, p. 126, No. 584.

183. Æ sestertius. 71 C.E. Mint of Rome. 24.90 gr. 34/35 mm.

Obverse:

Laureate head of Vespasian to right. Border of dots.
Legend, around from lower left: IMP(erator) CAES(ar) VESPASIAN(us) AVG(ustus) P(ontifex) M(aximus) TR(ibunicia) P(otestas) P(atriae) P(ater) CO(n)S(ul) III.

Reverse:

Victory, half-draped, standing to right,. with left foot on helmet, writing on oval shield hanging on palm-tree with seven branches and supported by her left knee. On right, seated captive Jewess, weeping and leaning head on left hand, with right hand on knees.
Legend, around from lower left: VICTORIA AVGVSTI; in exergue: S C.

Bibliography: *Mattingly* II, p. 126, No. 582.

184. Æ as. 71 C.E. Mint of Tarraco. 10.90 gr. 26/27 mm.

Obverse:

Laureate head of Vespasian to left. Border of dots.
Legend, around from lower left: IMP(erator) CAES(ar) VESPASIAN(us) AVG(ustus) CO(n)S(ul) III.

Reverse:

Victory standing to right on prow, draped, with wings spread behind; raised right hand holding wreath; left hand holding palm branch resting on left shoulder. Border of dots.
Legend, around from lower left, VICTORIA NAVALIS (Naval Victory); in field flanking: S C.

Bibliography: *Mattingly* II, p. 193, No. 792.

185. Æ denarius. 72/73 C.E. Mint of Rome. 3.30 gr. 16/17 mm.

Obverse:
Laureate head of Vespasian to right. Border of dots.
Legend, around from lower left: IMP(erator) CAES(ar) VESP(anianus) AVG(ustus) P(ontifex) [M(aximus) CO(n)S(ul) IIII].

Reverse:
Victory, draped, striding to right, holding palm branch in left hand, resting on left shoulder; right hand raised, placing wreath on legionary standard at right. Border of dots.
Legend, around from lower left: VICTORIA AVGVSTI.

Bibliography: *Mattingly* II, pp. 13–14, Nos. 75–77.

186. Æ quinarius. 73 C.E. Mint of Rome. 1.55 gr. 15/16 mm.

Obverse:
Laureate head of Vespasian to right. Border of dots.
Legend, around from lower left: IMP(erator) CAESAR VESPASIAN(us) AVG(ustus).

Reverse:
Victory, draped, striding to right, holding wreath in raised right hand and palm branch in left hand, resting on left shoulder. Border of dots.
Legend, around from lower left reading outward: VICTORIA AVGVSTI.

Bibliography: *Mattingly* II, p. 17, No. 91.

187. Æ as. After July 1, 73 C.E. Mint of Rome. 11.30 gr. 27 mm.

Obverse:
Laureate head of Titus to right. Border of dots.
Legend, around from lower left: T(itus) CAES(ar) IMP(erator) PON(tifex) TR(ibunicia) P(ostestas) CO(n)S(ul) II CENS(or).

Reverse:
Victory, draped, standing to right on prow, with wings spread rearward, holding wreath in raised right hand and palm branch in left hand, resting on left shoulder. Border of dots.
Legend, around from lower left: VICTORI(a) AVGVST(i); in field flanking: S C

Bibliography: *Mattingly* II, p. 155, No. 675.

188. Æ as. 74 C.E. Mint of Rome. 9.95 gr. 28 mm.

Obverse:
Laureate head of Vespasian to left. Border of dots.
Legend, around from lower left: IMP(erator) CAESAR VESP(asianus) AVG(ustus) CO(n)S(ul) V CENS(or).

Reverse:
Victory, draped, standing to right on prow, with wings spread rearward, holding wreath in raised right hand and palm branch in left hand, resting on left shoulder. Border of dots.
Legend, around from lower left: VICTORIA AVGVST(i); in field flanking: S C.

Bibliography: *Mattingly* II, p. 161, No. 705.

189. Æ denarius. 75 C.E. Mint of Rome. 3.40 gr. 15/18 mm.

Obverse:
Laureate head of Vespasian to right. Border of dots.
Legend, around from lower right, reading outward: IMP(erator) CAESAR VESPASIANVS AVG(ustus).

Reverse:
Victory, draped, standing to left on prow, with wings spread rearward, holding wreath in raised right hand and palm branch in left hand, resting on left shoulder. Border of dots.
Legend, around from lower left:
PON(tifex) MAX(imus) TR(ibunicia) P(otestas) CO(n)S(ul) VI.

Bibliography: *Mattingly* II, p. 31, No. 167.

190. Æ as. 77/78 C.E. Mint of Lugdunum. 9.90 gr. 26/27 mm.

Obverse:
Laureate head of Vespasian to right. Border of dots. (Globe at right tip of neck.)
Legend, around from lower right: IMP(erator) CAES(ar) VESPASIAN(us) AVG(ustus) CO(n)S(ul) VIII P(atriae) P(ater).

Reverse:
Captive Jewess, weeping, draped and veiled, seated to right on armor, head leaning upon left hand and right hand on knees; before her, round shield and two spears. Behind, palm-tree with five branches and two bunches of dates. To left, three oval shields, round shield, and two spears. Border of dots.
Legend, around from lower left: [IVDAEA] CAPTA; in exergue: S C.

Bibliography: *Mattingly* II, p. 210, No. 845.

191. Æ as. 77/78 C.E. Mint of Lugdunum. 10.80 gr. 27 mm.

Obverse:
Laureate head of Titus to right. Border of dots.
Legend, around from bottom: T(itus) CAES(ar) IMP(erator) AVG(ustus) F(ilius) TR(ibunicia) P(otestas) CO(n)S(ul) VI CENSOR.

Reverse:
Captive Jewess, weeping, draped and veiled, seated to right on two round shields, head leaning upon left hand, right hand on knees; behind, palm-tree with five branches and two bunches of dates. To left, two round shields and oval shield, spear, two helmets, and armor. Border of dots.
Legend, from lower left: IVDAEA CAPTA; in exergue: S C.

Bibliography: *Mattingly* II, p. 213, No. 864.

192. *AV* **aureus. Mint of Rome. 79 C.E. 6.60 gr. 19 mm.**

Obverse:
Laureate head of Titus to right. Border of dots.
Legend, around from lower right, reading outward:
T(itus) CAESAR IMP(erator) VESPASIANVS.

Reverse:
Trophy, comprising cuirass, helmet, round shield, and two crossed spears.
Below, in front of trophy, captive Jew kneeling to right with hands bound
behind back. Border of dots.
Legend, around from lower left: TR(ibunicia) POT(estas)VIII CO(n)S(ul) VII.
Despite the fact that there is no accompanying legend, this type belongs to
the "Judaea Capta" series.
This example is unique, although there is, in the British Museum, an identical
example in silver (*Mattingly* II, p. 46, No. 258). It was struck before Titus
came to the throne. The present coin was found in a hoard of gold coins
recovered from the sea off Caesarea Maritima. This type later became the
standard "Judaea Capta" design under Titus.

no. 193

no. 180

IMPERIAL ROMAN COINS COMMEMORATING THE VICTORY OVER JUDEA AND BEARING THE NAME OF TITUS AS EMPEROR

193. *Aᵥ* **aureus. 80/81 C.E. Mint of Rome. 3.40 gr. 19/20 mm.**

Obverse:

Laureate head of Titus to right. Border of dots.
Legend, around from lower right, reading outward:
Legend, around from lower right, reading outward: IMP(erator) TITVS CAES(ar) VESPASIAN(us) AVG(ustus) P(ontifex) M(aximus).

Reverse:

In center, trophy, comprising helmet, cuirass, oblong shield on each shoulder, and greaves below cuirass; flanked by seated captives, facing outward; captive on right (male?) with hands bound behind back; captive on left (female) draped and veiled, resting head on left hand, with right hand on knees. Border of dots.
Legend, around from lower left:
TR(ibunicia) P(otestas) IX IMP(erator) XV CO(n)S(ul) VIII P(atriae) P(ater).

Bibliography: *Mattingly* II, p. 230, No. 36.

194. *Æ* **denarius. 80/81 C.E. Mint of Rome. 3.40 gr. 19/20 mm.**

Obverse:

Laureate head of Vespasian to right. Border of dots.
Legend, around from lower right reading outward:
DIVVS AVGVSTVS VESPASIANVS.

Reverse:

Victory, draped, striding to left, with wings spread rearward, holding oval shield in both hands over trophy with crossed greaves; below, in front of trophy, Jewish captive kneeling to left with bowed head. Border of dots.
Legend, in field flanking: EX S C.

Bibliography: *Mattingly* II, p. 243, No. 112.

X. DENARII OF HADRIAN (117–138 C.E.)

Hadrian, with his planned renewal of the splendor of Greek culture and his anti-monotheistic attitudes, symbolizes another turning-point in the history of Eretz Israel. Its independence was lost with the destruction of the Second Temple in 70 C.E., but it was Hadrian's victory over Bar Kokhba and his founding of a Roman colony in Jerusalem (where legionary veterans were settled) which really put an end to the aspirations of the Jews – now largely dispersed beyond Judea.

In the Bank of Israel Collection, there are three silver denarii of Hadrian, depicting the goddess Victory in various forms. It is difficult to date Hadrian's coins precisely, as he served three periods of consulship, the last beginning in 119 C.E. We have only one other hint as to their dates: following the suppression of the Bar Kokhba revolt (135 C.E.), Hadrian was made *Imperator* for the second time. Two of the present denarii (Nos. 195 and 196) were probably struck before the Bar Kokhba war, whereas the third appears to have been issued subsequently, and may even commemorate this very victory.

195. Æ **denarius. 119/122 C.E. Mint of Rome. 2.85 gr. 17/18 mm.**

Obverse:
Laureate head of Hadrian to right. Border of dots.
Legend, around from lower left:
IMP(erator) CAESAR TRAIAN(us) HADRIANVS AVG(ustus).

Reverse:
Victory standing to right with wings spread upward, draped, holding trophy, comprising cuirass, helmet, and two oblong shields in both hands. Border of dots.
Legend, around from lower left:
P(ontifex) M(aximus) TR(ibunicia) P(otestas) CO(n)S(ul) III.

Bibliography: *Mattingly* III, p. 266, No. 212.

196. Æ **denarius. 128/132 C.E. Mint of Rome. 3.40 gr. 18/19 mm.**

Obverse:
Laureate head of Hadrian to right. Border of dots.
Legend, around from lower left: HADRIANVS AVGVSTVS P[atriae] P[ater].

Reverse:
Victory, draped, seated to left on stool, holding wreath in slightly raised right hand; left hand holding palm branch resting on left shoulder. Border of dots.
Legend, around from lower left: CO(n)S(ul) III.

Bibliography: *Mattingly* III, p. 293, No. 428.

197. Æ denarius. 134/138 C.E. Mint of Rome. 3.10 gr. 17 mm.

Obverse:
Laureate head of Hadrian to right. Border of dots.
Legend, around from lower left: HADRIANVS AVG(ustus) CO(n)S(ul) III P(atriae) P(ater).

Reverse:
Victory (as Nemesis), draped, striding to right; right hand raised; left hand holding branch downward. Border of dots.
Legend, around from lower left: VICTORIA AVG(usti).

Bibliography: *Mattingly* III, p. 335, No. 757.

no. 196

XI. CITY COIN ISSUES

Throughout the eastern part of the Roman Empire, the central authorities permitted cities to issue bronze coins so as to promote commerce through additional supplies of coinage from local sources. Not all cities minted coins, however, and not all of those which did began doing so at the same time; nor did their issues end at the same date. We do not know what principles governed the conferment of minting privileges on cities, but it is clear from the coins themselves that all the larger cities of that period did issue coins.

In Eretz Israel, city coins were in circulation more or less simultaneously with the Jewish coins, although most of the city issues are from the late first century C.E., until mid third century C.E., when the minting of bronze coinage was no longer worthwhile, the metal of such coins exceeding their face value.

Coins are often the only source for the history of certain cities. From what is depicted on them we can learn about the architecture of local public buildings, about the deities worshiped thereabouts, and about the army units stationed there. The legends can also often reveal the political status of a particular city within the framework of the Roman Empire – whether these be "autonomous" cities, cities of refuge, or "colonies." Many of the obverses bear portraits of the current emperor. Most probably, the cities were obliged to follow this practice, but it would also have served as an expression of goodwill indicating loyalty to the emperor.

Some of these city coins are dated from the founding of the particular city; this is not always based on the actual date of founding, but rather on the date when the city was granted its important status, or on which some other outstanding event occurred.

1. COLONIA AELIA CAPITOLINA

Hadrian's project for Colonia Aelia Capitolina – the name of Jerusalem over a period of several hundred years from the end of the Bar Kokhba war until shortly after the Arab conquest in the seventh century C.E. – was completed after the suppression of the Bar Kokhba Revolt. The city was rebuilt along Greco-Roman lines and was populated with legionary veterans. Of the temples dedicated to the Roman gods, the most important was that erected on the Temple Mount and dedicated to the Capitoline triad, Jupiter, Juno, and Minerva; this is the temple depicted on the first coins of Aelia Capitolina.

The city issued its own coins from 135 C.E. until the reign of Valerian (253–260 C.E.). From these coins the city's character as the garrison of an occupation force is evident; symbols of the Sixth and Tenth Legions are noteworthy. They also depict the gods worshiped by the city's populace (freestanding or within their temples). As with other colonies, so here the coins are not dated but the portrait of the emperor on the obverse serves to place them within the general chronological framework.

198. Æ small bronze. 138–161 C.E. 5.55 gr. 15 mm.

Obverse:
Laureate bust of Antoninus Pius to right. Border of dots.
Legend, around from upper right: IMP(erator) CAES(ar) ANTONINV(s).

Reverse:
Flying eagle to right on thunderbolt. Border of dots.
Legend, below: CAC (Colonia Aelia Capitolina).

Bibliography: Hill, p. 94, No. 71; L. Kadman, *The Coins of Aelia Capitolina (Corpus Nummorum Palaestinensium* I*)*, Jerusalem, 1956, No. 35.

2. ASHKELON

As a city of the Philistine pentapolis, Ashkelon (Ascalon) was one of the most ancient centers in Eretz Israel. Its port was always an important link in international trade, and it retained its independent status as a city, enjoying good relations even with Alexander Jannaeus. Ashkelon began issuing its own coins in 104/103 B.C.E., and it was the only city in this country which had the privilege of minting silver tetradrachms, for a short period during the second half of the first century B.C.E. The series of Ashkelon coins came to an end under Maximinian (235–238 C.E.).

The coins of Ashkelon are quite common; the imperial portraits are rather primitive, executed in a local manner typical of the city, and this is the only case of a city maintaining three types in three denominations for so extended a period: Tyche, the city goddess, on the large bronze; Phanebalos, the sword-waving war god, on the medium bronze; and a galley on the small bronze. Other designs also occur, such as a prow, double cornucopia, the Dioscuri, Poseidon, and the local goddess Derketo (Atargatis), to whom a *temenos* was dedicated near the city – a kind of sacred park with a pool containing sacred fish. There are also several designs in which Egyptian influence is visible, such as a square temple with four gates and a god (both in Egyptian style) and the goddess Isis. The coins of Ashkelon are mostly dated and the year of their minting is readily ascertained. The city's mint-mark was a dove.

199. Æ large bronze. 151/152 C.E. 17.70 gr. 26/27 mm.

Obverse:
Laureate bust of Antoninus Pius to right. Border of dots.
Legend, around from lower left: ANTWNINOC [CE]BACTO[C].

Reverse:
The goddess Derketo draped, with crescent on head, which is turned to left; holding dove in left hand and resting right hand on scepter. She stands on a triton who holds up a cornucopia in both hands. Border of dots.
Legend, around from lower left: ACKAΛWN (Ashkelon). In field, right below, date: ENC (Ashkelon, 255 [of the city's era, 151/152 C.E.]).

Bibliography: *Hill*, p. 130, No. 194.

no. 199

3. DORA

Dora, modern Tantura, was beyond the limits of biblical Eretz Israel, lying within the territory of Phoenicia. The Hasmoneans, however, brought it under Jewish control until the days of Gabinius. Its first coins were issued in 64/63 B.C.E. and the series continued until the reign of Elagabalus (218–222 C.E.).

The era of the city, as its coins reveal, dates from 64/63 B.C.E. The designs include the figure of Dorus, the city's legendary founder, Tyche, and a galley. In complete inscriptions the city is described as "Dora the Holy, City of Refuge, Autonomous, Ruler of the Seas."

200. Æ small bronze. 2.05 gr. 15/16 mm.

Obverse:
Head of Tyche to left, wearing turreted crown. Border of dots.

Reverse:
Galley to left, with eight oars and high aphlaston; cabin on deck. Border of dots.
Legend, above in two lines: ΔWΡΙΤWN/BAP (of the Men of Dora, 132 [of the city's era, 75/76 C.E.]).

4. NEAPOLIS

Neapolis – the "new" city (whence, in Arabic, Nablus) – was founded by Vespasian in 72/73 C.E. near ancient Shechem; Vespasian honored the city by granting it his family name, Flavia. Like its ancient predecessor, Neapolis was the urban center of the Samaria region, and it issued large quantities of coins from the reign of Domitian (82/83 C.E.) until that of Volusianus (c. 254 C.E.). Mount Gerizim, the Samaritan center, was the emblem of the city and as such appears on most of its coins, from the time of Antoninus Pius onward. In consequence of the Bar Kokhba war and the suppression of monotheism, the Samaritan temple on the mountain's summit was replaced by a temple dedicated to Zeus Hypsistos ("the Highest"). In the days of Philip the Arab (244–149 C.E.), the city was raised to the rank of Colony, and its coinage then became the most variegated and pleasing in its types throughout the land. The coins of Neapolis bear dates of issue from the founding of the city up to the beginning of the reign of Marcus Aurelius (161/162 C.E.).

no. 201

201. Æ medium bronze. 211/217 C.E. 7.00 gr. 21/23 mm.

Obverse:
Laureate bust of Caracalla to right. Border of dots.
Legend, around from lower left: AVTO(κρατορ) KAI(σαρ) ANTΩNEINOC

Reverse:
Serapis standing with head turned to left, wearing kalathos on head, half-draped, with right hand raised and holding long scepter in left hand. Border of dots.
Legend, around from lower left: AVP(ηλιας) ΦΛ(αουιας) NEACΠOΛ(εως) CYP(ὶας) ΠAΛ(αιστινης)

Bibliography: *Hill*, p. 58, No. 86.

5. NYSA-SCYTHOPOLIS

Nysa-Scythopolis – Beth-Shean – is first mentioned in the Tell-el-Amarna Letters of the 14th century B.C.E. During the Hellenistic period, it held an important position and under Gabinius it was removed, together with other cities, from the territories of the Hasmoneans and attached to the Decapolis. It was the only city of the Decapolis lying west of the Jordan river.

Nysa-Scythopolis first began minting coins during the reign of Caligula (40 C.E.), but the era designated on the coins is the Pompeian, which began in 63 B.C.E. The last of its dated coins are from the period of Gordian III (238–244 C.E.).

The name Nysa, commemorating Dionysus' nurse, points to the fact that this city was once a center of the Dionysian cult. This finds expression in many of the city's coins, which depict Nysa with the infant Dionysus on her knees, Dionysus as a youth, and the like.

202. Æ medium bronze. 176 C.E. 22/23 mm.

Obverse:
Draped bust of Lucilla (daughter of Marcus Aurelius) facing right, with hair knotted behind. Border of dots.
Legend, around from lower left: ΛΟΥΚΙΛΛΑ ΑΥΓΟΥϹΤ(α).

Reverse:
Tyche wearing turreted crown, standing to right, with right foot treading on a river god; left hand holding cornucopia and right hand raised, leaning upon long scepter.
Legend, around from lower left: ΝVϹΑ ϹΚV ΤΕΡΤ. ϹΕΠ (crude inscription): date flanking; ΘΛϹ (239 [of the city's era, 176 C.E.]). Pierced.

no. 202

6. GAZA

Gaza was the most important coastal city in the southern part of the country, and most of the Greco-Phoenician coins from the southern coastal strip were probably minted there. Hellenistic conquerors, both Ptolemaic and Seleucid, did not overlook this city and minted their royal issues there; Alexander Jannaeus conquered it in 96 B.C.E. This city inscribed the Pompeian era (starting in 61/60 B.C.E.) on its coins, but did strike coins even prior to Jannaeus' conquest bearing the legend: "Of the People of Gaza." The last of the city's coins were issued in the days of Gordian III (238–244 C.E.). Most of its coins are dated and in the reign of Hadrian a new era, dating from the year of his visit there (130 C.E.), appeared alongside the older one.

The coinage of this ancient Philistine city depicts gods whose origins go back to earliest Greek times – deities such as Minos, Marnas (a local form of Zeus), and the goddess Io. The city goddess, probably identical with Tyche, is called "Gaza," a personification of the city. The mint-mark on the coins of Gaza is: ⅄.

203. Æ medium bronze. 219/220 C.E. 11.10 gr. 23/25 mm.

Obverse:

Laureate bust of Elagabalus. Border of dots.
Legend, around from lower left: AVT(οκρατορ) K(αισαρ) M(αρκος) ANTONEINOC

Reverse:

The goddess Io standing on left, facing right, draped and extending hand to personified Gaza standing on right, facing, and turning her head to left. Gaza wears a turreted crown and holds a cornucopia in her left hand; at her feet, a calf. On lower right, rectangular countermark depicting head (Janus?). Legend, around from upper right reading outward: ΓΑΖΑ (Gaza); in exergue: Ε.ΠC (280 [of the city's era, 219/220 C.E.]). On left, mint-mark: ⅄

Bibliography: *Hill*, p. 166, No. 140.

7. PANEAS

Paneas (modern Banias), near the source of the River Jordan, was known as Caesarea Philippi from the era of the tetrarch Herod Philip I (see above, pp. 45–46). The original name stems from the cave of the god Pan, from which the waters of the Jordan still gush forth. The earliest literary mention of the city dates from the Hellenistic period, when Antiochus III defeated the Ptolemaic general Scopas nearby in 198 B.C.E.; in this battle, Egypt permanently surrendered its territories in Eretz Israel, which now came under Seleucid control. The population of Paneas was mainly non-Jewish and Herod the Great erected a temple there in honor of Augustus. The city was the capital of several rulers of the Herodian dynasty – Philip (who renamed it Caesarea Philippi in honor of Augustus), Agrippa I, and Agrippa II (who in his turn renamed it Neronias in honor of Nero).

The period during which it issued coins was rather brief – from the reign of Marcus Aurelius until that of Elagabalus, i.e., only some sixty years. Most designs on the coins of this city relate to the cult of Pan, who is depicted standing (apparently after a statue which once stood in the opening of the cave or in one of the niches still to be seen adjacent to it). There are also representations of Pan within the cave and of his pipes on the city's minor issues.

204. Æ medium bronze. 161/180 C.E. 12.10 gr. 24/25 mm.

Obverse:
Laureate, bearded bust of Marcus Aurelius facing right. Border of dots.
Legend, around from lower left: ΑΥΤ(οκρατωρ) ΚΑΙΓ[. . . ΑΝ] ΤWΝΙΝ
ΟΣ ΣΕΒ(αστος)

Reverse:
Pan standing nude, leaning on tree-stump, and playing his pipes. Border of dots.
Legend, around from lower left: ΚΑΙΣ(άρεια) ΣΕΒ(αστὴ) ΙΕΡ(ὰ) ΚΑΙ ΑΣΥ
(λος) Η ΠΡ(ος) ΠΑΝΕ(ίω)
flanking: ΡΟΒ (172 [of the city's era]).

Bibliography: F. De Saulcy, *Numismatique de la Terre Sainte*, Paris, 1874, pp. 316–317 (Marc-Aurèle), No. 1.

8. SEPPHORIS

Sepphoris (Zippori) is located in the central Galilee. It is mentioned by Josephus in connection with events in the days of Alexander Jannaeus (first century B.C.E.). Sepphoris was the seat of one of the five *synedria* of the Hasmonean government under John Hyrcanus II, based on the division of Gabinius. It was also the capital of Herod Antipas early in his reign. There were many non-Jewish inhabitants and, during the First Jewish War against Rome, the city opened its gates to Vespasian, who is described on several of the city's coins as "Peacemaker." The religious feelings of the Jews were still respected in the city's series of coins under Trajan, and their designs are similar to those of Neapolis under Domitian, featuring the wreath, palm-tree, caduceus, and two ears of corn. After the Bar Kokhba Revolt, the name of the city was changed to Diocaesarea. This forms a parallel with the substituted Roman name for Jerusalem Aelia Capitolina, as far as the components are concerned: *Aelia* stems from Hadrian's family name and *Caesarea* honors the emperor; Capitolina represents an aspect of Jupiter, head of the Roman pantheon, while *Dio* signifies Zeus. After the bestowal of this new name, the coins of the city bore such titles as "the Holy," "City of Refuge," and "Autonomous." The coin series of Sepphoris begins under Vespasian, before his accession to the throne (68/69 C.E.), and ends under Elagabalus (218–222 C.E.). None of the coins of Sepphoris bear any date.

205. Æ small bronze. 68/69 C.E. 13.90 gr. 19/20 mm.

Obverse:
Border of dots.
Legend, in center: large S C; around, from lower left: ——— HNO EIPHNO ΠOI (Peacemaker); above S C: CEΠΦΩP (upside-down) (Of the Men of Sepphoris).

Reverse:
Circle surrounded by wreath tied at bottom, with leaves in groups of three. Border of dots.
Legend within, in five lines: LIΔ/NEPΩNO/KΛAYΔIOY/KAICAPO/C (14th year [of the reign of] Nero Claudius Caesar).

Bibliography: M. Narkiss, in *BIES* 17 (1953), pp. 108–120 (Hebrew).

9. CAESAREA MARITIMA

During the fourth century B.C.E., in Persian times, a Phoenician anchorage named Strato's Tower stood on the later site of Caesarea. Only under Herod the Great was a great harbor erected here – Sebaste – with the adjacent city known as Caesarea, both named in honor of the Emperor Augustus. In time, this city became the capital of the Provincia Judaea and, from 6 C.E. onward, it was the seat of the Roman administration in Eretz Israel. Until the First Jewish War, Caesarea's Jewish population was quite large, though after the heavy casualties suffered at the outbreak of the disturbances it declined; we know, however, that even as late as the early Byzantine period there was a movement of Jews from the southern cities to Caesarea, and many persons are noted in the Talmud as its inhabitants (R. Yose bar Ḥanina of Caesarea and others). Vespasian granted Caesarea the status of a "colony" and, since it was the first city to be granted this distinction, he renamed it "Colonia Prima Flavia Caesarea Augusta" (The First Flavian Imperial Colony, Caesarea). After the Bar Kokhba war, the city received another honor – the title "Metropolis Provinciae Syriae Palaestinae" (The Metropolis of the Province of Palestinian Syria).

The sand-dunes of Caesarea have yielded thousands of coins, mainly from later periods, i.e., the Late Roman, Byzantine, and Arab. But the operations of the mint at Caesarea first began at the start of the first century C.E., when the Roman procurators began minting their coins there. The first coin issued in the name of the city was minted by Agrippa I (No. 55). Various groups of coins found in this country which lack the name of an issuing authority (such as those bearing a rudder or anchor) were most probably also issued at Caesarea by the Roman administration. This latter authority also issued all the city's coins in Flavian times (see Nos. 164–175).

City coins were first issued by Caesarea under Nero in the fourteenth year of his reign (67/68 C.E.), and from then until the reigns of Trebonianus Gallus and his son, Volusianus, in 254 C.E. During this period the city issued many coins and it is not surprising that there are so many different types. Tyche occupies an important position among the designs, but other gods also appear, such as the Imperial triad, Demeter, Dionysus, and others. During the third century C.E., one particular type of coin was minted in vast quantities, depicting an eagle with wings spreading to meet above and forming a circle within which stand the initials: SPQR (Senatus Populusque Romanus), "The Senate and Roman People."

206. Æ **large bronze. 217 C.E. 17.40 gr. 28/31 mm.**

Obverse:

Laureate bust of Macrinus to right. Border of dots.
Legend, around from lower left:
[IMP(erator) CAE(sar) M] ACRINVS AVG(ustus).

Reverse:

Roman eagle facing, with head turned to left and wings spread forming circle above. Border of dots.
Legend, around from lower left: COL(onia) [PRI(ma) FL(avia)] AV(gusta) [F(elix) C(oncordia)] CAESA[R(ea)]; within circle SPQR.

Bibliography: L. Kadman, The Coins of Caesarea Maritima (*Corpus Nummorum Palaestinensium* II), Jerusalem, 1957, No. 77.

no. 206

10. RAPHIA

Raphia (Rafa), the southernmost coastal city of the land, is well known from various sources dating back to the first millennium B.C.E. Detailed information about this city is available again only in the first century B.C.E., when it was conquered by Alexander Jannaeus, although it was later severed from the Hasmonean kingdom by Gabinius (c. 60 B.C.E.). The coins of Raphia are relatively late, from the second and third centuries C.E., spanning the reigns of Marcus Aurelius (161–180 C.E.) and Philip the Arab (244–249 C.E.). As with the coins of Nysa-Scythopolis, Dionysus occupies an important place on those of Raphia, where he is depicted as an infant in the arms of Tyche, and also as a youth. On other coins of this city there are depictions of Zeus, Apollo, Artemis, and other deities.

207. Æ medium bronze. 230/231 C.E. 13.95 gr. 23/24 mm.

Obverse:
Laureate bust of Alexander Severus to right. Border of dots.
Legend, around from lower left:
ΑССΛΩ (ΑVΤ(οκρατωρ) Κ(αισαρ) Μ(αρκος) ΑVΡ(ηλιος) СΕΟV(ηρος) ΑΛ[ΕΞΑΝΔΡΟС])

Reverse:
Dionysus, nude, but with cape draped over left shoulder and arm, standing with head turned to left; left hand raised, leaning on thyrsus (wand) and right hand raised, holding wine jug. On lower left, panther looking up. Border of dots.
Legend, around from lower left: QC ΙΕΡΑ ΡΑΦΙΑ (Raphia the Holy, 290 [of the city's era, 230/231 C.E.]). Both the script and the spelling are corrupt and hard to decipher.

no. 207